MW00942992

Finally Free
"He's Just To Forgive Us"
2nd Edition
Copyright 2018
Tamu Lane

Cover art by Tamu Lane

Editor: Tamu Lane

FOR INFORMATION CONTACT:
Tamu Lane
856-296-4229

Dedicated to all the women and men who lost their lives due to domestic violence. To those survivors of sexual abuse striving to move forward and past their pain. To those struggling with an eating disorder and fighting to be whole. I salute you all in your fight and your struggle to be set free.

Acknowledgements

The Lord Jesus Christ: I am so thankful to you Lord for all your many blessings. You are my refuge and my strength and I love you with all of my heart and soul. Amen.

I am grateful for my parents that raised me to be independent, kind and loving towards others. Thank you mom and dad!

.

Table of Content

The End
Wounded
Freedom
Red Flags
Knowledge Is Power
More than Physical

Scene 3 164
Free
The Beast
What is Bulimia?
Confusion
The Struggle
Middle Ground
Frenzy
The College Years
The Beginning of the End
Hope
The Funeral
Confession
The Treatment Center
The Walk
Altered Mind
Scare Tactic
Who Can See What I See?
Tie Breakers
History
Today
Affirmations
Healing Process
Scene 4 228
My New Day
Referral...234
References.............…...................................224
About the Author.........…...............................237

Welcome To My World

Introduction

Welcome to my world. Be ready to learn that my world was not filled with joy, but it was actually a world filled with pain. Are you ready to take this journey with me as you read and discover the trauma that one girl experienced? Buckle up your seat belts, because it is going to be a bumpy ride, but if you stick it out, I can promise you that you will be blessed at the end. How do I know, well it turns out for the good of the Lord who loves me. Let's get ready!

So, why did I decide to tell my story? For this one simple reason: people are wounded. No matter what their background consist of, people are wounded walking around with invisible scars. Having those invisible scars are such a common correlation between many individuals. Living with suppressed emotions has caused many of us to live in a way that is self-destructive. When people are in a self-destructive mindset it is hard to see clearly. It's hard to see what you know is not healthy but we accept it because it's your way of validating that you are not worthy of anything great. Therefore, people find themselves in destructive relationships, unable to adequately parent and accepting whatever the world has to offer. With this thinking, people tend to criticize and blame themselves for what has happened in their lives. Being their best critic for situations that were out of their control.

Before we were formed in our mother's womb, God knew us. Before we were even a twinkle in our parents' eyes, God knew us. He knew what mistakes we were going to make before we made them. He knew the hardships and trauma that was going to be committed against us. He knew it all. He also gave us a way out of all of the trouble that He knew we were going to get into ourselves. He gave us Jesus! The one that died on the cross for us and freed us from our sins. Jesus is the blessing that we have in knowing that we will have peace throughout this journey of suffering, and trials and tribulations. Jesus is the promise that God gave to us.

While beginning to write this book I began to ask "God, why did I have to suffer the way that I did?" What I realized was how can I be a witness to another human being if I have never experienced life myself? Testimonies are what bring souls to God. We are people that need concrete evidence to persuade us. We need to know that someone has experienced what we are going through for our statement to hold any weight. That's why testimonies are so important to share. When one person shares their pain without embarrassment, it opens the door for others to share their pain as well. To be set free is why I am telling my story. Someone else needs to be able to share their story without embarrassment and heal their wounds. Who better to counsel someone who's an alcoholic than someone who has been freed from alcoholism? All the degrees in the world cannot add up to real life experiences.

I want to share with you this journey through some of the pain and sufferings that I had to endure, along with sharing how I overcame many of my fears. Even to this day, I continue to work on myself to conquer things that have overtaken me. Hopefully, through this book, someone can learn how to release those things that have been taunting them and move on peacefully with their lives.

Growing up I always felt abnormal. As if there was something extremely different about me. I could never put my finger on it, but I knew that I was not like other people. I always had a hard time finding my place in this world. I never knew just how different I was until now. I always felt like others were judging me. What I've learned is that no matter how different you are in God's eyes you are perfect. If you get nothing else out of this book, please always know that God is still God and he shall remain the same yesterday, today and forever more. We are His children and God is the only judge. So we have to use our past as our strength and move forward in blessing others.

One of the biggest lessons that we have to learn is that through our afflictions God can and will create good to come out of them. Pain causes us to become closer to God. When we are going through something traumatic, our prayer lives tend to increase tremendously. We don't want to hurt, so we began to ask God to free us from the pain, not realizing that God is trying to change something within us. Spiritual growth comes from affliction. Humility comes from affliction. I remember always hearing the saying, "No Pain, No Gain." The statement of no pain, no gain is also true with God. Without pain how can we grow spiritually and learn humility? Yes, pain hurts and many times it can be crippling but what I do know for sure is that it will not kill us but only strengthen us if we hold on and not give up. You nor I can afford to give up on life even through all of its trials. Reason being we were born to be a blessing to someone, in some way, for some reason and if we give up on life, then we nor they will ever have the opportunity to experience the gift that we have to give to them.

Tamu Lane

Scene 1

Dirty Girl

Throughout this book, you will find out that I am very inquisitive and I tend to ask many questions. Questions are what provides us with the information that we need to go forward on our journey. So let's begin: Have you ever met someone that has been raped? Someone that has been defiled, abused, split open and used? Someone that has been incarcerated in their minds due to all of the blame, guilt, and shame that tormented them? Yes? No? Not sure? Well if you have, pay attention to what I am about to tell you. If you have not, listen up more attentively. And if you're not sure, well just take a look at me. Interestingly enough some of you might be able to take a look at yourself. There are no distinct features of a sexual abuse survivor. We don't have a specific type of sound coming out of our mouths. As a matter of fact, our looks are not distinct from your own. We breathe, talk, look, feel, touch, laugh, and have dreams just like you. We sing, dance, smile, frown, yell, scream, and have failures just like you. We are compassionate, loving, serving, and successful just like you. We have desires and needs just like you. We have struggles and challenges just like you. But with all of that, there's a special connection among children like us. When we find out about others who have experienced similar traumas in their life, some of us tend to bond in our likeness and cry out to one another. We seek similarities in our situations in hopes of finding solitude. In our reaction to being sexually abused, some of us withdrawal and hold it in. We are seeking to heal and therefore we use coping mechanisms which many times come in the form of drugs, alcohol and for many of us, food.

Others act out, not knowing how to deal with their emotions and the reality of what happened to them.

That tomb of darkness composed of misery and sorrow for oneself can become so large and unbearable to handle. Many times a child's mind is not stable enough to take in all of that pain that has been placed upon them. Let me explain that statement: of course as children the trauma is done to them so there is no question about them taking the pain. The problem is that many times they cannot deal with the pain and therefore they rebel. Children rebel in so many ways. Some of this rebellion can come in the form of underage drinking, cigarette smoking, use of marijuana, snorting or smoking cocaine, popping pills, cutting, suicidal thoughts and this is only naming a few. And what happens in many cases is that if that child does not seek to heal early they tend to grow in age but not in maturity and therefore the same type of behaviors are shown. They continue to rebel on a much larger scale, giving themselves permission to act out.

So if so many of our children are being affected by sexual abuse how come we continue to ignore it day after day, week after week, month after month, year after year? Why is our society so afraid to confront sexual abuse? Why are we closed to the idea that there could be a family member abusing our loved ones? Why do we protect family members instead of our children? Why do we continuously re-victimize those that are suffering? When is the world going to see the tears in our children eyes? When is the world going to see the fears that exist within our children's souls? When is the world going to get real about fighting for the rights of those that are sexually abused? When?

Every day there seems like there is another case of sexual violence against a child or an adult. And every day a perpetrator is getting off with a slap on his hand. What is it going to take for us to wake up and realize that violating another human being is not right, not acceptable and just plain old inhumane?

The title of this first chapter is called Dirty Girl because that's how I felt. Like a dirty girl! I felt Smelly! I felt Stinky! I felt Disgusting! I felt worthless! I felt every unimaginable, hateful word that anyone could begin to even think of in their minds. And this is a feeling that many children today and at one time in their lives have felt. So, because of this, I decided to reveal my past of childhood sexual abuse to the world so that we as a society will continue to understand the importance of fighting for one another. There are many survivors of sexual abuse that have passed away and can no longer speak their truth, so we must fight and speak for one another. We have to believe, not disregard. We have to put our fears aside so that we can support those around us that have been touched by sexual abuse as a child, with the hopes of becoming healthy adults. It's time to open our ears, and our eyes and sees what's right in front of us.

In the stages of adolescence, there are so many children struggling to deal with being sexually abused by a family member or a close friend of the family. Their coping mechanisms are shown in the form of acting out in school and at home. Our family systems along with our school systems have become so detached that they are pushing medication as soon as a child is a little disorderly. Instead, they should be trying to find the root of the problem. When a child experiences this type of trauma, it's hard to communicate one's feelings. They will cry out many times for help, but too often no one ever seems to hear them. Often people don't hear children when they're crying out. We are prone to shut them up, making comments about their behavior. These types of responses many times, make them feel worse than they already did. Children will tell you most of the time what's going on if you only pay attention to them and listen.

The Day I Died!

Childhoods are interesting! Conflicting many times in the mind. Great on one end, traumatizing on the other end. I felt as if I was living on both sides of my brain at the same time. One side I was excited and happy, exploring the world of childhood. On the other side, I was depressed and traumatized, hating the fact that I was born. So conflicting in my head is what it was like growing up as a child in the city of Camden, New Jersey. The city where children were playing in the street, grandma sittings on the porch, entrepreneurs making a living on the corners, kids playing street ball on the side of houses, and a squad of teenagers up at the yellow store playing Ms. PACMAN. Man, this was the life to the innocent eye, but to the open eye, it was rough. Living in the city taught me a lot about people and life itself. It taught me about who I could and could not trust. It provided me with a roadmap twisted and yet straight in so many ways. You couldn't help but grow up influenced in both directions. You got to see both sides of the coin and depending on your individual mindset at that time you could have been influenced by either side, no matter how you were raised. But what I know for sure is that living in the heart of the city can and will produce strength, but it does not always produce the type of strength that is needed for every situation that one comes up against for example sexual abuse.

Well now that I talked about how great it was to live in the city, let me tell you about how great it was to live at 47 North 24th Street. It was so many of us together, loving on one another, raised by love. First, there were the 4 of us: my mother, father, brother and myself. But then there were the rest of my mom's six brothers and sisters (3 uncles and three sisters) and they had children, and their children along with my brother and I were all raised to love one another as brothers and sisters. Wow! We had a ball together. Some of my cousins lived right across the street from us and some lived 30 minutes away. Even though they lived in the country we stayed connected. There were also times where some of us lived in the same household which created an even stronger bond between many of us. It was something to see and experience. Love in all of its glory. We always had each other's back and in that, I always thought that we could trust one another. Never any questions ask, just pure love. We were taught that family means everything and that you never turn your back on them. Our elders taught us that you always have something to feed your family no matter when they show up. You always extend courtesy and kindness. So for me, the word family is a word that revolves around unity, protection, and guidance. But what I learned so quickly as a child was that sometimes in dealing with family those words have no meaning. It's just all talk.

As a child, I dreamed in color, very imaginative thoughts. Dreams of rainbows flowing through my head. Dreams of being away floating on a cloud. Dreams of being a little girl safe and secure. Dreams! That's all they were. It was just too much going on in my thoughts because of what was going on with my body. It was just too much for any child to have to bear, but I did. I had no choice. All of the choices were made for me. Could you believe it, they made the choices for me. I had no say in the matter. I was so young when things started happening to me. Eight years old! Eight years old! Eight years old! What were you doing at eight years old? Playing catch a girl, get a girl or were you playing dodgeball? Well at eight years old I was being raped. Yes, raped! Having my body detached from my soul was my reality at eight years old.

Safety first, was very important to my parents, therefore they never allowed me to stay the night anywhere that was not a relative's house. Their concerns were valid. The only problem was that the whole stranger danger ideal went out the window this one evening. It was more like family danger is what we should have been looking to investigate. As children, we are so groomed to look out for those lurking around the corner being watchful, which we should but there's a new predator in town. And the reality is that this predator is not new to any family, just ignored.

What is Incest? Incest is where someone is raped by a blood relative. For many years people practiced this way of living as if it was ok but it's sickening to think that having sex with your child, your brother, your sister, your niece, your nephew, your cousin or your grandchild is alright. The damage that it does to an individual is so devastating. It's horrifying because there are so many twisted emotions that are involved. For the victim, the relationship can become sort of a love/hate relationship because it's hard to disconnect your emotions towards your loved one that raped you. It's a fight that many individuals struggle with on a daily basis and I am seeking to help as many as I can to be set free through my journey of healing.

Did you know that I am an Incest Survivor? Well, I am! The very first time I was at a place that I thought was safe. That my parents thought was safe. Who would ever imagine that something as horrible as rape would have taken place at a relative's home? I should have been kept free from any harm or danger. Eight years old! How could I protect myself? I could barely wipe my nose well enough, let alone protect myself from a predator. When I think back on it, it amazes me because there were other kids in the house. The older kids were watching the younger kids because our parents went out for the evening. We were all very close so we enjoyed spending time together and during our time together someone took advantage and misinterpreted the meaning of closeness. I can remember being in the room with everyone but feeling a sense of loneliness. We were playing a game which got out of hand and tag I was it. I went into the other room scared and anxious. I shut the door and sat on the bed. When I realized that the door was not shut I stood up to close the door and he came in behind me. I thought that we were all playing a game but it turned out to be something totally different.

Playing this game was not something that I signed up for and I wanted to leave but was forbidden to do so. Without many words, he grabbed me by the arm and pulled me into the closet. I didn't understand what was going on, but because he grabbed me I tried to pull myself away from him. When he got me into the closet he shut the door. I don't know if it was fear kicking in or just my imagination but I can remember this awful smell that reeked from his body. He then pushed me against the wall and began to pull down my pajama pants. As I tried to push him away again he grabbed me harder and harder, so eventually, I stopped. I did not scream because I was scared. Before I knew it he began to force his penis inside of my vagina and at that moment every ounce of innocence was gone. He just kept going and going and he would not stop. All I could remember thinking was how painful it was and wishing that it would end. Then my thoughts began to repeat why me, why me, why me? What did I do to deserve this? When he finished he had the audacity to say to me that no one is going to believe me so he suggested that I kept my mouth shut.

Have you ever been in so much pain that you couldn't even cry? It is the kind of pain that kills people because they have no way of getting rid of it and no way of letting it out. It is the kind of pain that no pain reliever could ever cure. Being raped was the first time that I wanted to die at that very moment. I saw no purpose for living, no purpose of existing. I felt extremely alone and unprotected. How could that happen to me? How could he do that to me? What was he thinking? I was eight years old, scared, alone and fearful of him. How did I know that this was not going to happen again? Was he crazy enough to do this again?

When he finished taking my innocence, he left me there by myself, all alone as if I wanted it or deserved it. All I could do was curl up and hope that someone would come and help me, but they never did. I did wonder if they knew what was going on. Did they set me up? I wondered! Because absolutely no one came to my rescue. Even if they did not know what was going on, no one came to check on me, therefore I couldn't help but wonder if someone else knew what was happening to me. So I stayed in that closet for a while before I decided to go into the bathroom and tried to clean myself up. I kept using toilet paper to help with the bleeding because I knew of no other way. I had to grow up fast that day to survive. I felt extremely dirty. Dirty! Dirty! Dirty! Embarrassed! Embarrassed! Shamed! Yucky! Stinky! Dead! I was dead inside. He had cum in me and it felt sticky and smelt horrible. I DIED THAT DAY! Baby girl, Mookie, Boogie, which is what they called me, died that day. Everything in me shifted in a way that I can't quite explain but what I do know is that it shifted for the worse. I was so afraid to tell anyone because I did not want to take the blame for something that I did not do. He did this to me. He RAPED me! So why couldn't I tell anyone? Where did that information come from that if I told anyone it would not have been believed? I wish I knew and I wish that I had the strength to tell someone. Maybe it would have protected me from further experiences of being raped, but I guess, I will never know.

Keeping this secret damaged me as a child and into adulthood for many years of my life. Being raped left me in a state of confusion and turmoil. It left me not knowing how to deal with my feelings and being unable to love others. I didn't know how to live after that and being so young it just distorted my whole perception of men in general. I became extremely private and wrapped up in my world full of anger, confusion, hate, and self-pity. Men became the forefront of my hatred. There was a sense of disgust lying within me.

I HATED ME! Imagine hating yourself. You can't get away from self. As an eight-year-old child, I should have never known the depth of what hatred resembled. The care's that were on my shoulders were larger than life itself. What was I to do? And how was I to deal with it? These are questions I could not answer.

Guess what, he did it again! This time I was home in Camden. As I mentioned previously there were two sides of how I lived: the fun side and the depressed side. On this one evening, we were all playing in the schoolyard around the corner from my house. We were just playing around like we did many times. At first, we were playing hide and go seek which was always fun. As that game started to wind down we were trying to decide what to do next. We decided to gather around the back of the school near the little brick building that was used for trash. Even though I knew he was with us playing, I was just having a good time with everyone else running around like kids do. A few minutes after everyone began to walk back around the corner he grabbed me by my arm and told me not to leave. Because we were all still running around being loud no one paid attention to him nor I. So as they were moving in one direction he was pulling back towards the trash building. He then pulled me inside and pushed me up against the wall, pull my pants down and raped me again.

The family that I was supposed to trust raped me again. He kept pounding me and pounding me, so I began to scream but no one heard me. He kept trying to put his hands over my mouth but I was crying and yelling. Eventually, he let me go because I wouldn't stop being loud. When he let me go I ran back around the corner with everyone else but the strange part about it was that no one asked me where I was. I was one of the youngest ones running around and yet no one was looking for me. No one! How is that? And then he comes around the corner and no one asked us where we've been? Everyone was oblivious and in their own world. So much for watching after the babies. We were just left to ourselves to survive as best as we could.

We put too much trust in things and in people instead of putting our trust in God. We trust family as if they could never do any wrong but we must be just as watchful with family as we are with strangers if we want to protect our children. Because what reason would anyone have for hurting a child in such a way that violates their every being? There is absolutely no reason that anyone could provide. There is never a reason for taking something so precious and delicate from a child or from anyone else for that matter.

Being sexually assaulted is truly devastating. It can ruin vast parts of your life, take away your childhood as you know it to be, take away your innocence and just completely leave an individual in limbo. We have to reach our youth and teach them how to protect themselves. Let them know that they have a voice. They deserve to be safe.

Desperation! Anticipation! Annihilation! These are the feelings that go through the mind of a suicidal child. Desiring to end their life so that the pain would end. Discontinuing those thoughts of hatred amongst oneself. Desperate! Desperate! Desperate to die! Oh, how this pain must end. The anticipation of committing suicide is a fear all within its self but you want the pain that you feel to go away so bad that it seems to be a way to free oneself. It seems worth doing because when you are in that state your mind tells that no one else will be able to hurt you ever again. Your mind tells you that it's time to be free and the only way to be free is to remove yourself from the world. It's such a distorted thought process but at the time it seems so real to that individual. It seemed so real to me. A wounded, broken child, full of fear, shame, and sadness.

For many people, it's hard to imagine why someone would want to take their life. It's hard to imagine pain so intense that it can place you in a state of no longer wanting to live. No longer wanting to breathe. No longer wanting to exist. But my existence lies in fear, hopelessness, and disgust for oneself and when that is illuminated nothing else matters in the mind of someone that is suicidal. Being raped caused me pain beyond belief. There were two sides to that pain. I felt the physical pain and the mental pain. The physical pain was so bad that my body was going into a convulsion. And the mental pain made me feel insane as if I was going out of my mind. So when you have these two combined it is a recipe for destruction. Because of these two entities spewing within myself, there grew a sense of hatred within myself, therefore I saw no need to continue on living.

The very first time that I tried to kill myself was so surreal. The thought scares me to think about what I tried to do. I can remember being home and feeling burdened with the world on my shoulders. I couldn't deal with the pain that existed within me. In the bathroom cabinet, there were razors and prescription drugs. At this young age in my life, I don't remember taking much of anything other than a pill for a headache maybe. While in the bathroom I kept staring off into space. I was confused and disheveled in my mind trying to understand what I was feeling inside. So as I sat there on the bathroom counter I began rocking back and forth contemplating on taking my life to end the pain. After a while, I went into the cabinet and pulled out a razor blade. I sat back on the counter, rolled up my sleeves and with the blade in my other hand I began crying profusely. I was scared of the pain that I was about to inflict on myself but I was also scared to continue on living. I continued to sit there rocking back and forth until I got up the nerve to cut my wrist. Within a matter of minutes, I decided to make an attempt to cut my arm. The pain was so unbearable. I never felt anything like that before. I started to bleed in which I became extremely frightened that someone was going to find out, so I threw the blade in the trash and flushed the toilet to cover up being in there so long. I ran to my room and cried for hours, waiting for the pain to stop. The physical pain was horrible to deal with and the mental pain was just as bad. It just seemed crazy that I would do something so irrational to myself. I was afraid to live. I just wanted to die. Just that simple.

Life seemed a little different after that first attempt. I had to look at this scar that I created and hid from the world. The mental pain lasted so much longer because I was reminded every day due to the scar on my wrist. How does a mind so young even know what to do? How does a mind so young even begin to understand the magnitude of what occurred? How does a mind so young, so innocent become so violated and disturbed, to believe that the only way out for me was to die? And how come no one saw my destruction? How come no one was paying close attention to me? I was all alone in my head and it was a lonely space and I felt desperate. Every time it felt as if I had no other option. Wow! So young, yet so disrupted in my thoughts. Who could have ever imagined that this was taking place in the mind of such a young child, but it's happening every day. Children are trying to figure out how to survive in such a hostile world. And I was trying to figure out how to survive in a world that I perceived hated me.

Bullied! Yes, I was bullied! Along with being sexually abused I was being bullied just about every day. I didn't feel like I had the space to tell anyone about anything that was happening to me. I felt so alone. When I was in elementary school I would be shoved into the bathroom with the door being kicked up against me. Constantly being pushed around and threatened that I was going to get my butt kicked. It was just one thing after another and I never felt that sense of security. Nowhere felt safe for me. Home, school, nowhere! Where was I to go? What was I to do?

When a person experiences a sense of extreme loneliness it can play tricks on your mind. Creating disillusioned thinking which could make a person believe that they are worthless. And this belief provided me with the ammunition that I needed to try and take my life. One time, in particular, I remember feeling so depressed and angry that I found a bottle of pills in the bathroom cabinet and I swallowed a handful of them. After I took them I began to get very scared that I was going to die and began to force myself to throw up. I continued to stick my fingers down my throat hoping to find relief. I was not very successful in making that happen. After some time, I began to get extremely tired and all I could remember was waking up hours later in my bed. I just couldn't understand why it was so hard for me to take my life. Why didn't God just let me die? I was more frustrated than anything because nothing seemed to work. I either didn't have the boldness to cut deeper or the pills just didn't affect me enough to kill me. Why was I here to begin with? What was the purpose of even creating me? What did it serve? I would ask God these questions over and over again with no answers, so I thought.

After some time I began to have this extreme fear of dying. I would constantly think about death having these distorted thoughts. Sometimes when I would lay in my bed at night I would get so scared that someone was going to kill me by coming up the stairs and stabbing me to death. And because my bedroom was right in front of the stairs, I felt like someone could have gotten away with it because of everyone else being busy. I hated the night time because it was so frightening. It was lonely and the house would always make noise.

Sometimes I would try to make excuses to sleep in my mom's room on the floor and sometimes it would work and other times it would not. It was hard growing up as a child because I never felt safe telling anyone my struggles. I didn't think that they would have understood. So I just kept slowly dying inside, feeling alone, feeling awkward, feeling like an outsider.

As I just mentioned my bedroom was directly across from the stairs and there was a time where the bed was facing the doorway. So I would lay there looking out towards the hallway thinking about ways to kill myself. This did take up a lot of my thoughts. So one day I thought to myself that if I only could accidentally fall then I could break my neck and then all of the pain would be gone. Because in the mind of a 10-year-old if I broke my neck I would have been dead. And I could remember thinking about this for days on days. Every night the same thought would come back. It got so intense that I began to replay my steps to see if this would even work. So I decided to place myself at the top of the stairs playing out the scenario in my head crying intensively. I was trying to get up the nerve to jump and when I thought I was ready I would freeze up and sit at the top of the stairs. I would sit there and cry and then I would try it again to no avail. Finally, I decided to jump and as I fell I banged and bruised my body. Throwing myself down the stairs was so crazy to do, but think about it. Imagine being eight years old and having someone rape you over and over and over again. Imagine someone threatening you, putting fear in you, and then raping you again. I was so wounded inside and all I wanted was some relief. I was being raped, bullied and made to feel like an outcast. So at this point in my life, I would have tried anything to die.

I wish it would have stopped here but it didn't. I kept trying but nothing worked. Nothing held to be true. And every time I tried, the more depressed I got, so I began to find relief in alcohol and other means of being free. No one ever taught me about survival, therefore I found my way to survive which ended up in years of destruction and chaos.

Peaceful! Quiet! Serene! That's what it was like in our backyard. We lived in the big yellow house that had a fence around it. We were fortunate enough to have a huge yard as well. As a child, I spent a lot of time on our back porch. I would sit there, and my imagination would run wild in order to protect me from my reality. The porch itself had a lot of space which made it easy for me to play with my things. It was my thinking place, my place of serenity. For me I felt closed from the world, making it a safe place. Even though I lived in the heart of the city I felt like no harm could ever come to me while in the circumference of my palace.

Imagine how I felt when all of my security came crashing down. It was somewhat surreal. I was sitting on the porch playing like children do and minding my own business when my neighbor which I will call Sam decided to jump over the fence and sit next to me. Where we lived the houses were adjoined except for the last three towards the corner. These houses were separated by a fence. The fence was very low, which made it easy for anyone to climb over. When he came and sat next to me I thought nothing of it because I knew Sam very well. There was no fear within me towards him. At the time I had to be about ten years old and he was at least in his early 20's. While he was there I continued to play as if I was alone. After some time he began to talk which annoyed me. I was not too interested in being around anyone at that time. He was actually invading my space and I wanted him to go away but for some reason he wouldn't leave. He just sat there. After some time he asked me where everyone was and I just shrugged my shoulders. The one-sided conversation continued on his part and I pretended as if he was not even there and proceeded to play as usual.

I was hoping that if I ignored him long enough that he would leave. While he was talking, he asked me if he could play with me and I told him no. He continued to try over and over again to engage himself in what I was doing but at no point would I allow him into my world. I noticed as I began to look at him out of the corner of my eyes that he was getting irritated with me. Next, he decided to put his hand on my thigh and began rubbing it up and down my leg, getting very close to my vagina. My heart began to pound out of my chest. So I asked him what was he doing and proceeded to push his arm off of my leg. He started laughing and then placed his hand back on my thigh. Soon after that, he placed his hand on my little 10-year-old breast. I was flat chested with no form whatsoever but that didn't stop him. While he was rubbing my chest he stated that it was important for the both of us to keep this as our little secret because if anyone found out we could both get in trouble. At first, I froze up, being in complete shock of what was going on and in fear of being hurt again. Once I was out of that state of shock, I began to yell but he placed his hand over my mouth and told me to shut up or else. For me or else meant being hurt. He then removed his hand from my mouth and because of his threat of harm I did not try to yell again. He then began to unbuckle his pants and pulled out his penis. I refused to look at him but he kept yelling at me to look at what he was doing to himself. He told me that he wanted me to imitate his actions and stroke his penis up and down.

I refused, so he grabbed my hand and forced me to stroke him. After what seemed like a lifetime, he then picked me up and sat me on his lap. At that very moment was when I began to put up a fight. All I could think about was being hurt in the closet and in order for this not to happen again I needed to run quickly. So somewhere within me I found the courage and ran as fast as I could around to the front of the house. No one was outside at the time so I proceeded to run through the front door and straight up the stairs. I was afraid of this man because I had no idea of how far he would go to get what he wanted. When I ran upstairs I went into the bathroom and headed straight for the window to see where he went. He was back on his side of the yard standing by the gate as if nothing had happened. I wished that Sam was a stranger because at least there would have been a better chance of me not seeing him again. I felt like I was going to be tormented by him for the rest of my life until I gave him what he wanted.

The following day when I saw him he tried to have a conversation with me as if nothing happened. I was very frightened of him and wished that he would leave me alone. The worst part about it was that he become closer to my family. I felt like if I told anyone that I would be partly to blame and only make the situation worse. There were a few other occasions where this man tried to push himself on me but it only got as far as the first time. Eventually, he did leave me alone.

Uh! But whom else did he attack?
I guess I will never know.

Why do we blame ourselves? Blame usually is staring us right in the face. Making sense of an action is hard to come by therefore we find fault in our minds. Finding fault with self is a normal sign of coping. It is hard to see the truth and think about it because the truth is scary. It's real and it's honest, which we tend to run from because of the pain that it causes. The connection with this is that truth hurts and it makes you face the problem head-on.

Sexual abuse can leave a person in a state of guilt and shame. You feel guilty that you did something wrong and shame kicks in because you belief that you are partly to blame. Especially when you haven't told anyone, you continue to feel more pain because if it's a secret, you must have done something wrong. Not true!

There is also that need of wanting to know why it happened, which will never change the action that occurred. There is a deep yearning in others to find out why someone has done what they have done to them. This consumption of the brain takes away that person's power and healing process. It's wasteful energy! I say all of this because if a person gives a reason, what makes it true and would it change what they have done to you? The answer is no, therefore we must focus on what can benefit our healing and move forward.

Renewing our minds have to take place so that we can believe and understand that abuse was not our fault. When we are violated as a young child we must understand that those actions were placed upon us and our innocence was taken.

The White House

Every 98 Seconds someone is Sexually Assaulted in the United States. (5)

As I think about every sexual assault that occurred, most of them happened close to home. I was taught about staying away from dark allies, not speaking to strangers and being cautious about walking at night alone. But what about our closeness to home. Many times it is just as dangerous as the streets that we walk on every day. Where is our right to safety and security? Isn't home where the heart lies but yet so many children are raped right there in the compounds of their heart.

So let me tell you about the White House! What comes to your mind when you think of these words: The White House? My first thought was that big beautiful building in Washington, D.C. The place that houses the President of the United States of American. The place where justice and equal rights were created for every American that is living and breathing. But this White House that I am speaking about is far beyond that thought process. The White House that I am speaking of holds trash and anything else that you could create in your mind. This White House was a shed in our backyard that was closed in by a fence. Nothing fancy, just a shed for our convenience. There were many occasions where we had to go back there, whether to put out the trash or for some other reason. No matter what time it was, if trash needed to go out or if mommy needed something from back there, we would go and get it. No big deal, right? Well on this one particular evening I had to make a trip to the White House to retrieve something. Honestly, I have no clue what it was but it could have been anything.

So, let me set the stage for you: A few weeks before this one particular incident there was a neighbor which I will call Mark who would constantly harass me to sleep with him. He was once again much older than I and very forceful in his speech towards me, but nothing would ever transpire. I was afraid of Mark just by his appearance and the way in which he talked to me. He always had this tone that was very soft but hard at the same time due to the language that he would use. During this time I was around 11 years-old and he had to be about 19 years old. He was the younger brother of the individual that sexually assaulted me previously.

During this one evening, I was on my way to the shed. Our yard was pretty big, so from the time that I reached the back of the house to the time I reached the shed, he could have seen me coming. As I was proceeding to go towards the shed and got to the doorway, a hand reached out and grabbed me by my shirt. I couldn't understand how or why Mark was even in there in the first place but I guess it didn't matter. I say that it didn't matter because knowing the reason would have never changed what occurred inside the White House that evening. My heart was pounding out of my chest. I had no idea who was pulling me in at first until I got my bearings and when I recognized his face I was filled with fear. I thought about his constant advances towards me to have sex and here we were all alone. Mark wasted no time assaulting me. He pinned me up against the wall and told me not to move. I did what I was told out of fear. Next, he began to pull his pants down and grabbed me by my neck in which I began choking. I tried to swing my arms to get away but to no avail, I did not succeed. He then shoved me by my head and forced me to perform oral sex on him. It was one of the most humiliating moments of my 11-year-old life. Wanting to die at that very moment.

A few seconds later I threw up all over him and myself. He got mad at me and pushed me onto the floor in which my head hit the wall of the shed. Next, I heard a yell which saved me. I heard my mom calling my name and in an instant, I was able to run out of their and into the house. As I entered the house I ran straight upstairs, hoping that no one would see the vomit that was all over my clothes. I headed for the bathroom and washed my mouth out with soap. It had a horrible taste, but it was better than what I had just experienced. As I sat there in the bathroom, I could not understand why this kept happening to me. What was it about me that made these people dislike me so much to inflict this kind of pain on me? I just wanted to die. Tired! Completely tired! I was only 11 years old but yet the pain I felt was astronomical. And something in me told me that I could not tell anyone. I was still afraid of being accused. Mark was convinced that no one would believe my story.

Afterward, Mark would look at me every day with this sadistic expression on his face. He seemed to have no feelings about what he did to me. I had never sensed a feeling like this which was stronger than anything that I had ever felt before. I know now that it was a feeling of rage and hate fuming from within me. I remember having visions of committing murder. I truly wanted to kill him. Why would anyone do that to a child? He damaged me and I wanted to damage him by any means necessary.

Intoxicated

Alcohol and drug use is raging amongst our youth today. It was huge when I was a child and it continues to grow even larger now. It is so easily accessible, like buying candy from the corner store. It seems almost normalized. But I wonder, how do we change this epidemic? How do we help the youth see that there is a better way to cope with the trauma that has occurred within their lives? Honestly, is it even possible? I believe it is. It has to be, that's what hope is all about.

When I looked at myself in the mirror all I saw was disgust and shame for that little girl. That little girl was not worthy of anything wonderful. I didn't recognize who she was and personally, I didn't care. I didn't think anything about myself. I was junk! I was worthless! I was nothing! I didn't love anything about myself. I hated me! I felt useless! I had no purpose. Coping with life began to get hard. Up to this point, my only means of coping has been trying to take my life and that hadn't worked, so I needed a new fix. Wow! For the first time, I fell in love. He was gentle and kind. He didn't judge me. When I needed him he was right there ready to assist. Who was this amazing guy? Well, he was known to me as Alcohol. Since nothing else seemed to work so far I found something that helped to take the pain away. I turned to drinking at the age of 12. It was easy to get. There was a neighbor that lived a few doors down from me who was known as the neighborhood alcoholic. I don't know how it started but she became my best friend. I began spending a lot of time with her because I knew that she would allow me to drink. She didn't ask me any questions.

She was older than I was and since she didn't mind I took advantage of the opportunity. I started drinking beer just about every day and noticed that the more I drank the more the pain went away. The feeling that I got from drinking took me to another world. A make-believe land filled with happiness and laughter. But what I noticed was that I began to want more. I was in need of a greater high so after a while beer was not enough so I began to drink liquor, which made me feel even better. The more depressed I got, the more I drank. It became like a daily regimen, which became easy to hide.

Then I found myself wanting to feel even higher. So I began to smoke marijuana, which became part of my coping regimen. Smoking marijuana put me in a calmer state. I began to rely on that feeling of peace and wanted to feel this way every day, so I did what I had to do for me. Getting this drug was easy because it was right at my fingertips. I was able to get it for free every time. The use of drugs and alcohol was how I learned to cope with life. I was constantly crying out for help but no one seemed to hear me. I screamed and I screamed but no one heard me. I acted out in many ways. My grades were deplorable, my attitude stunk but yet no one heard me. So I kept smoking and drinking as much as I could to find some type of rest within myself. On a regular basis, I was fighting from within not to kill myself, so the use of substances help to keep me on this earth.

By the time I was 13, I would have considered myself an alcoholic and pothead. I could not get through many days without it. And as I look back, those days that I was not able to consume either substance I remember feeling edgy, moody and irritable. Having these emotions caused me many problems throughout my young life, not realizing that the substances that I used caused many of my issues in dealing with other people.

New Year's Eve! I was 14 years old and drunk as usual. My mom was not home because they were out partying celebrating the New Year. So we took advantage of the time and a few of us were hanging out around the neighborhood late that evening drinking and getting high. Getting intoxicated was a common thing that occurred amongst us, but because it was New Year's Eve we drank even more than usual. After a while we all decided that we were hungry, so we took a walk to the store which was a few blocks away from where we all lived. When we got to the store there were people hanging outside staring at us but we thought nothing of it. We were all drunk and high out of our minds so we were oblivious to what was going on around us. As we left the store none of us paid any attention to people following us. That evening I had on a long leather trench coat, a pair of gold name earrings, and EK glasses which were very popular back in the day. We were almost home when a couple of guys jumped out from nowhere and asked me, what time is it? I went to look at my watch and as I was looking up he said that it was time for me to give up my coat. He had a gun and a pair of brass knuckles on his hand. Seeking to rob me, he took my coat and my earrings, and the other guy was chasing my cousin down the street. Everyone else was just running. In a matter of time, my high went away. I was so scared because I didn't know if this guy was crazy enough to use that gun but he did use the brass knuckles hitting me upside my head. For the first time, I wanted to live and not die which was a strange feeling. But this did not stop me from drinking, it only increased my desire to want more.

Drinking! Smoking! Drinking! Smoking! Drinking! Smoking! That was my life. My grades continued to decrease but no one asked me why. I was seen as a defiant child. Defiant! Lazy! Selfish! Angry! That's what they saw in me. That's how I saw myself. What was I to do? The life I wanted was removed from me and I had nothing to give. So with that, I was ready to jump, but they pulled me back.

It was 1990, prom night. I was not your typical beautiful girl. I was what some considered as the ugly duckling. I had no self-confidence. I was always picked on, being made the brunt of everyone's jokes. I was the ugly girl with big lips and a big fat body. That's how my peers referred to me. But anyway, I decided to attend with a few of my girlfriends. There was one guy who agreed to meet me at the prom and take pictures together, but I knew that he did it out of sympathy. So throughout the evening, we had a good time, but I couldn't wait to get to the after party so I could drink. That was all I was thinking about the whole time we were there. After we had left the prom we attended the after party at a local hotel. I can remember drinking one drink after another, after another, after another. I became popular for being intoxicated. I had to be intoxicated wearing that powder blue puffy dress with powder blue shoes. Why didn't somebody tell me that I looked a mess? Anyhow, after some time I guess I got bored and decided to climb out onto the ledge of the balcony. We were on the 3rd floor and there was nothing but cars and concrete beneath me. I began swinging back and forth with one foot on the ledge and the other up in the air, and I was holding on to the railing with one hand. As I felt my foot slipping I felt a hand grabbing me and pulling me back onto the balcony.

If I had fallen I would have dove straight into one of the cars beneath me. One would have thought that this would have scared me enough to stop, but as I landed on the balcony all I could do was laugh.

At no time did I have fear in my heart of dying, which explains how drunk and high I was that night. I saw no end to this cycle and it just continued to intensify with no signs of slowing down.

Let me ask you: Are we watching? Are we listening? Are we paying attention? I don't' know. Listening is an acquired skill that everyone needs to possess but doesn't. I remember that old saying that children ought to be seen and not heard. In some cases that might be true but in many it is not. Children need to have the ability to express themselves when something is going on. They have to feel safe in speaking and recognizing that they are supported in all things. And being supported is a must so that our youth can learn how not to cope by using drugs and alcohol. Our youth are dying because no one is listening. What I have learned throughout my experiences is that we have to tell our children that it is alright to use their voice. We shove them away when they are screaming for help. We disbelieve them when they try to speak. I know all too well what these feelings do to one's soul. As adults, we must learn to communicate with our children so that they don't grow up feeling alone and abandoned. A long-term side of effect of feeling alone and abandoned can bring about negative coping skills because they don't have a positive outlet.

The great blessing of life is that we do not have to repeat our behaviors. We have the power to break the cycle. We have the power to use our voices. We can learn how to do things in a healthier way. We just have to find the strength inside of us to believe that we are worth it. Sexual abuse does not have to define who we are and what we do with our lives. Even though we were harmed, we do not have to live as a victim for the rest of our lives. We can become survivors and then thrive in this world.

A majority of child victims are 12-17. Of victims under the age of 18: 34% of victims of sexual assault and rape are under age 12, and 66% of victims of sexual assault and rape are age 12-17. (6)

As a young girl, their bodies tend to develop way before it catches up to their age. It can be embarrassing for her to receive unwanted attention by an adult male or woman. And depending on her level of maturity she will either be flattered and inappropriate behavior will be shown or she will be afraid and began to try to cover herself up.

For myself, I hated that my body was shifting. I was a tomboy and I wanted to stay that way. I would try to cover myself up as much as I could. I didn't wear tight clothing or anything that would reveal any extra parts of my body. It was embarrassing for me and I did not want any extra attention. Even though I didn't try, I still received negative attention in the worse way. Neighborhood men would start talking to me. They would make very suggestive comments about how I was developing. Some of them would make me offers to come and hang out with them. I would laugh due to being nervous and say no thank you. They would try to offer me things, thinking that I would sleep with them but once again I would always walk away laughing. Sometimes I was not always able to walk away so quickly without them rubbing up against me or whispering in my ear what they wanted to do to me sexually. I could never understand what they saw in me.

I wasn't suggestive, I didn't do anything to make them think that I was open to their sexual advances. So it boggled my mind constantly. Here I was a 14-year-old girl and grown men wanted to have sex with me. I could never understand their attraction to a child.

One particular man totally took me for a loop with is unexpected advances towards me. It was weird because at first, I didn't think much of it. He was one of my favorite cousins. I use to believe that he was kidding around and trying to make me laugh, which he did. Every time he saw me he would tell me how pretty I was and how nice I looked in my clothes. He always complimented me every time I saw him but it wasn't like, "hey you look nice." It was more like, "hey you look sexy and your boobs are getting bigger." My cousin was talking to me in this way, but still there was never fear in my heart for him. I always looked up to him as one of my big cousins, which made things even worse when he decided to rape me.

My family and I were on our way to visit some relatives for the weekend. We were excited to see them because it wasn't often that we got to visit their home. When we got there everything was going well. We were laughing, eating, joking and having a good time with everyone. After some time, I began to get tired and decided to go into my cousin's bedroom and take a nap. I was lying on the top bunk watching television when he came in to see what was going on. We chit chatted for a while and then I decided to just lay my head down and look at television. He then mentioned that he was also tired and should probably do the same thing. When he said that, I figured he was going to lay down somewhere else, maybe on the bottom bunk, but instead he climbed onto the top bunk with me.

When I realized what was going on, I quickly moved and began to climb down. He pulled me back onto the bed and stated that I didn't have to leave. As he climbed up on the bed and laid behind me he stated that he just wanted to lie down as well. I was very uncomfortable but I stayed.

I began to think about all of the sexual advances that he made towards me and I became worried. While lying behind me he proceeded to place his arm around my waist, not allowing me to move. In an instant, my heart starts beating fast. A few moments later he then put his other hand down my pants and began to touch my vagina. He repeatedly whispered in my ear that this would be our little secret. All I could think about was here we go again. He tried to kiss me but I kept moving my face away from him as much as I could. I tried to be as quiet as I could. He then took his hand out of my pants and began to pull his pants down. Afterward, he pulled my pants down. I was so afraid I could not move, even though inside of me I was struggling to stay still. He then rolled me over, placed his penis inside of me and commenced to rape me. A few moments later he loosened his grip off of my waist and I got up the strength to move away from him. I quickly jumped down off of the bed, put on my pants and ran into the bathroom. I guess everyone was still outside because no one came to the door and said anything. I stayed in that bathroom for a long time. I cried and cried continuously. I was in so much pain and relieving myself in the bathroom made it worse. I wanted to say something to someone but in my mind, I felt like they would either blame me or not believe me so I dealt with this by myself. Since we were there for a few days I had to see him several times and he acted as if nothing happened. Things were back to normal; as if he had a right to take what was mine.

I felt so alone. I was away with my family and yet I still had no security or safety. I was a mess. Wounded and angry again because this kept happening to me. I was raped and all I wanted to do was rest. He wasn't a stranger. He wasn't some crazy man off the street. He was my cousin, my flesh and blood and yet he hated me. Why else would he RAPE ME?

Manipulation

Manipulation! It's such a negative term that people use to get their way. It's not normal nor is it right. It's not right to treat someone as if they are only there for your benefit. It's not right to make someone feel like you are interested in them just for your gain. It's not right to be so selfish that you would threaten someone to get your way. It's just not right. I felt like I had been manipulated on many occasions because guys were looking out for their best interest, not mine and therefore I suffered.

I always wondered why people believe that they could have power over someone. Why they believed that their money could buy anything and anyone for the right price. I would never understand that. So, I had an encounter with someone who thought that they could do just that because of what they had. He was a big-time drug dealer who flaunted himself. Women would flock to him, one after the next. He had what many women were looking for, which was money and nice cars. He basically could get any woman that he wanted. He walked around like he owned the world and everything on it. For some reason, on this one particular day, he decided to disturb my life. I will call him Jesse. I just happened to be sitting on my front porch when Jesse came over to the side gate and began to make small talk. I didn't have much to say to him but he did pass the time. He was a guy that I didn't believe I should fear because I grew up with him. He was a good friend of my brothers and at one time he used to call me his little sister. So, as the conversation progressed I began to get confused. He was asking me questions about having sex with him. When I did not respond in the manner that he wanted me to, he then began to make accusations about my sexuality.

All of this came about because I would not give him what he wanted. So instead of going into the house, I listened to him go on and on about what he was going to do to me. And from there he threatened to start rumors about my sexuality that were false. When that didn't move me and get a response he then began to offer me bribes for sex. I was amazed that this man would go through all of this drama just to sleep with me. He could have had any women that he wanted, but instead he chose a 14-year-old child. I couldn't understand what this was all about. I told him to please leave me alone, but he refused to stop coming at me. At this point, I was tired and lost all respect for him. I could have walked away from the situation but I felt like I was safe on the porch. His threats of physical violence got worse. At this point I finally decided to walk away from him, hoping that he would forget about it and eventually leave me alone. It took a minute to realize that this man had lost his mind and that I didn't have to be bothered with him.

Later on, that day while I was walking to the store, Jesse saw me again and began to threaten me with violence. He would tell me that he knew girls that he could seriously hurt me. And when that didn't affect my demeanor he would threaten to do it himself. I didn't understand why this man continued to harass me. It just didn't make any sense. How does someone go from being a person's little sister to now someone that they desire sexually? I guess because he couldn't have me, he decided to force himself upon me which seems ridiculous but that's what happened.

That evening while I was home sleeping, I heard a noise outside my window which startled me. When I looked outside I saw that it was him telling me to come down now. I began to get very frightened. I didn't want my mom to hear him. After a few minutes he started to get louder and louder so to shut him up I went downstairs to see what he wanted. When I went downstairs I opened up the side window to talk with him. Immediately he grabbed me by my shirt, pushed me back and climbed through the window. As I was trying to move away from him, he pushed me down on the floor, pulled down my pants and raped me. He forced himself into my anus, with his hand covering my mouth. The pain was so excruciating that it felt like a tree being rammed inside of me. If I had a choice of being dead or alive at that moment, I would have chosen to be dead. Why was this grown man inside of me? Life wasn't all so beautiful then. For me, I had to stay focused and realized that this would all be over soon. My prayer was that hopefully, he would leave me alone now that he got what he wanted. I was more concerned about someone hearing us and coming downstairs. I felt like I would've been responsible for him being there in the first place because I was the one that opened up the window. When he was done, he pushed me down, pulled up his pants and quietly left the same way that he came. And I was left on the floor in pain.

At that very moment, I felt like I was in hell and that this was where I was going to be for the rest of my life. I questioned for a long time whether or not I was raped. I was in my bed asleep when he threw rocks at my window and I had a choice in whether or not to respond to him. I said to myself I could have told my mom or just ignored him, but I chose to go downstairs to see what he wanted. I felt like I had a hand in what happened to me. As I got older I realized that what happened to me was rape. The only reason I answered his call was to get him to stop, not to be raped.

A message to my rapists:

I hated you for a long time. I allowed you to take up so much of my time and energy to the point of exhaustion and depression. You took my innocence away from me without my permission. You were so focused on being in control that you snatched my life out from under me. That word control is so powerful and strong. It's hard to imagine that a person would do anything in their power to gain control over another human being, especially a child that had no power to hold up against you. Because of you, life has not been easy for me growing up, dealing with things such as low self-esteem, anger, and hatred for you and myself. Do you know what it is like to hate yourself? Living in the skin, day after day, that you don't want to live in and having no way out other than killing yourself. Every single one of you caused me this pain. For the majority of my life, I did not like who I had become because of you. How do you change what others have made you out to be? How do you find your true identity in this life? I had a hard time figuring out those questions. Then there was my sexuality. Why should that have been an issue for an eight-year-old? I owe that all to you. When I got older there were times when I wanted to confront some of you to try and get my questions answered. Questions like, what did I do to make you rape me? I know that this is probably something that you can't answer and that's okay. I thought that I could benefit from knowing why, but I was wrong. I began to seek God for healing in this situation because I knew no other way. And with His power, I was able to let go, move forward and forgive. You no longer have control over my life, my mind nor my well-being. I release you from my mind now and forever, giving myself permission to be set free.

Unintended Consequences

What does the research say about childhood rape victims and their response to the abuse of being promiscuous?

According to Harner (2016), the research shows the effects of trauma, specifically sexual trauma, on victims' physical, psychological, and social well-being was first explored in the early 1970s. Many times when this victimization occurs early in life, young victims may attempt to adapt by internalizing or externalizing the traumatic event. The research shows that many times girls are more likely to internalize victimization, which may result in depression, anxiety, and self-harm. They may engage in more risk-taking behaviors, including early sexual initiation, sex without contraception, unprotected sex, sex with multiple partners, and substance use. (7)

What was I searching for? Love? Attention? Could they give me what I was longing for? I placed myself in so many compromising and unsafe situations. Many situations where I could have lost my life. I was desperate for something. I was desperate for Love!

Chains Broken

Many times we seek answers and when we get them we are still in the same misery that we were in before we got what we had sought out for. What I have learned is that our healing is not in the why factor, but in God. Knowing why would never change the situation nor make it all better. Also, a person's explanation of why is not always the truth, so what's the purpose of knowing. I can honestly say that today I am no longer angry nor do I hate my abusers nor myself. It took me many years to be free from their chains. Chains that had me bound and I thank God that I forgave them. I don't have to accept what they did, but I did have to forgive them. They will no longer take over my mind or my spirit. They will no longer dictate who I am and what I am. And most importantly I will no longer feel like any of this was my fault.

In this book, I purposely created fictional names simply because this book is not about them, but about the women, men and children that have been hurting at the hands of molesters and rapists. It is time for people to heal and stop holding on to their past. Your past can kill you if you don't let it go. It can set a course for destruction if it's not released. As survivors of this horrible crime, we deserve a sense of peace and a clear mind to go forth through life in exploring all of the possibilities that the world has for you and me.
One of my biggest prayers to God was asking Him to help me forgive them totally. And that He forgives and restores them fully. And lastly, I asked him to teach me how to learn to forgive myself. Forgiving ourselves is just as important and can continue to keep us bound in sadness if we don't release it from our hearts and minds. Freedom is liberty!

Matthew 6:14-15

Jesus says, for if ye forgive men their trespasses, your heavenly Father will also forgive you: but if ye forgive not men their trespasses, neither will your Father forgive your trespasses. (3)

The word forgiveness is hard for many of us. It's not easy to do. It's one of those things that are more easily said than done. It is especially hard to do when you have to forgive those who have violated you. It's not simple to do, but it must happen. We can't be confused about whether or not we will forgive. In one period of my life, I had a hard time understanding forgiveness. Many times it didn't make sense why I was supposed to forgive such wretched men. I hated them from the bottom of my heart. There were many days where I wanted them dead. But everything changed when I allowed God to work in my life. God is pure love. You cannot get any purer than Him. And writing this book as an adult helped me to realize many things. God had forgiven me for so many things that were not worthy of His love. But even in my worst state he still forgave me with no questions asked.

I had to come to terms with the fact that forgiveness had to be given to those individuals that harmed me for many years. It was a hard pill to swallow. What I've learned over the years is that forgiving them was not for them but for me. When I walked in hate and anger it messed up my life. It made me depressed, which would force me into negative behaviors. What we as a people have to understand is that when we forgive others for what they have done to us, it frees us. It allows for us to live and be free citizens. When you forgive someone it is not about being their best friend or trying to patch up holes with them. It's about trying to patch up the holes within you and most importantly with God. The power of forgiveness is so amazing because it frees you from bondage. It gives you a sense of hope and many new possibilities in life. So we must allow ourselves to be free and not think that we're letting the other person off the hook if we forgive.

The Bible says that God takes our sins and remembers them no more when we repent. If our purpose in life is to be Godlike in our human form we must work hard to forget about all of the hurt that was placed upon us and moves forward. What I had to realize was that for me to be completely free from my past I had to forgive every single person that had ever violated me, abused me, and humiliated me. When you possess God's kind of love it doesn't matter what the other person feels towards you. God's love is not based on emotions.

Remember Mark! The White House! Well many years ago someone told me he passed away, so this allowed for me to make amends with him in my heart. Well what do you know, it was on Christmas Day, 2017 and we were in Downtown Camden feeding the homeless. We had many people come through our line because we were the only group out there that day. So as I was standing on the assembly line and placing chicken on people's plates, as I was looking down I heard my cousin whisper in my ear, "there is Mark". I said who, "Mark, she said". And as I looked up there he was standing right in front of me with a big smile. At that moment all I begin to think about was that I thought he was dead. But after that quick thought, I smiled back and I served him just like everyone else. The sad part about all of this was that he didn't even recognize any of us. Mentally he was lost but my job was to serve him just the same. I felt no pain, no hatred, and no sadness. Only sadness was for his current state of being and I prayed for him within myself. This was such a defining moment for me realizing that I did forgive him totally.

As survivors of sexual abuse, we must have the boldness and the courage to allow ourselves to heal. Within my journey of healing, there were certain steps that I had to take to come to the point where I am today. One of the very first things that I had to do was realize and accept the fact that this did happen to me and that I needed to make that huge decision to heal.

#1-Acceptance of the problem! No one could do this for me but me. When anyone decides to get healing, regardless of where the healing comes from, they must first and foremost admit that there is an issue going on. They must decide that they will not continue down this path but seek to heal instead. Once a person gets through this first stage I believe that the rest is smooth sailing. Like anything, the hardest part is admitting and once you admit the work begins and now you can grow.

#2- Anger! Another big part of the healing process is dealing with the anger inside of you. Anger is a natural feeling and one should not be afraid of it. It is extremely powerful, in that, it can eventually set you free. A person has a right to get angry at their abuser and they also have a right to let it go. Letting the anger go can allow you to move forward and not allow the negative pent-up energy to continue to fester inside of your being. There is nothing wrong with being angry. It's what we do with our anger that makes the difference.

Anger should send a person in a direction to want to make something happen for good, not for the worse. It should inspire a person to want to change. When a person's anger is released, it frees them to be open so they can conquer the world.

#3- Forgiveness! The next piece included forgiveness. I talked about this in depth previously. As stated it was a very important factor throughout my healing process, just as important as forgiving myself.

#4 Spirituality! And the most important factor to healing was seeking God in all of this. Knowing that there is a greater power than you and being able to call upon that name, "Jesus", for guidance and instruction is an awesome thing. We don't have to walk through this life alone. We have the opportunity to call upon a Father that is waiting to hear from us so that He can reach out and protect us. Trusting God and all His glory is what set me free and I am grateful for that today.

Now at the ripe age of 45, I have learned that even though it felt like God had left me in the past to deal with these things on my own, He truly was right by my side. For whatever reason, we all have to go through different things in our lifetime. I don't believe anymore that what I went through as a child was for no reason at all. It has shown its purpose in my life in many ways, for example as a therapist I have provided therapy to sexual assault survivors and domestic violence survivors. Having understood some of the feelings that others go through on a daily basis, I believe makes me even more equipped in aiding them in their healing process.

Words to the Hurting: There is somebody that is going through what I went through either right now or is a survivor, but is unable to move on and live a productive life. In telling my story, I know that what I went through will help someone else come back from destruction in their mind and finally be free. God created us to be powerful and strong and to stand for something other than our own needs and desires. So if releasing this information will help someone else, then so be it.

Please remember that it is never your fault, no matter what someone might say. Never be afraid to tell someone as I was, because no matter what the rapist says to you, telling someone will better protect you most of the time from future instances happening. Admitting to someone that you have been raped can be embarrassing, especially when you are an adult. People are going to judge you because they don't understand how someone could keep silent. But that's when you have to put those who judge you to the side. We have to take care of ourselves and allow for healing to take place, which should be the main focus. There are so many of us living with this thing bottled up inside, causing us so much pain. But the only way that we are ever going to be free is to forgive those that have hurt us, forgive ourselves and let it go.

Many years ago God showed me this book. And when I realized that I was going to have to talk about being sexually abused I was terrified. My mind was so tied up worrying about what others were going to think about me and how they were now going to perceive me. My thoughts began to twist and turn and fill up with fear. My mind was trying to convince myself not to do this book but I am glad that I did not allow for those thoughts to take over me. When I was able to get focused, God showed me that my story was bigger than just little old me and that people needed to be set free. If it weren't for Jesus, I would have never been able to forgive. He's my strength, my refuge, my ever-present help and He can be the same for you.

I don't know if we realize how much we have lost as survivors of child sexual abuse. It's as if we are grieving because something died within us. There is grief cycle that was created by Elizabeth Krueger-Ross and it looks something like this:

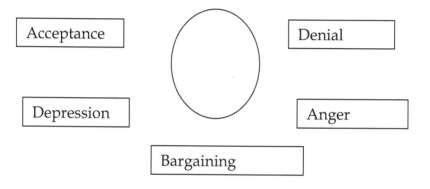

•**Denial**- At the core of denial is not accepting what actually happened.

•**Anger**- Angry about what has happened. Showing signs of frustration and humiliation.

•**Bargaining**- Many times this shows up as trying to make a deal with God. Wishing it never happened and trying to go backwards.

•**Depression/Withdrawal**- Coming out of denial and moving from bargaining can lead to depression. Having feelings of worthlessness, sadness, and disassociation.

•Acceptance- Accepting the fact that this really did happen so that we can move forward.

Now, this wheel does not move cyclically. It can move from one end of the spectrum to another. You can go from being in denial to depression, back to being in denial.

As I have spoken to a countless number of survivors, many of them won't even allow themselves to reach anger because it is seen in such a negative way. Many of them were taught not to get angry. It was not a good reflection of a young lady. But as I have taught them anger is a natural feeling and that is it well within their right to get angry about the violation that has been done to them.

So once again this wheel is an aid to help those that are victims as well as help those family members that are struggling with the abuse that has been perpetrated on their loved one.

The Truth about Sexual Abuse!

Sexual Violence refers to sexual activity where consent is not obtained or freely given. Anyone can experience sexual violence, but most victims are female. The person responsible for the violence is typically male and is usually someone known to the victim. The person can be but is not limited to, a friend, coworker, neighbor, or family member. (2)

There are many types of sexual violence. Not all include physical contact between the victim and the perpetrator (the person who harms someone else) – for example, sexual harassment, threats, and peeping. Other sexual violence, including unwanted touching and rape, includes physical contact. (2)

Statistics

Sexual Violence is a significant problem in the United States:

• Among high school students surveyed nationwide, about 8% reported having been forced to have sex. The percentage of those having been forced to ever have sex was higher among female (11%) than male (5%) students. (2)

• An estimated 20% to 25% of college women in the United States have experienced an attempted or completed rape during their college career. (2)

• Nearly 1 in 5 women (18.3%) and 1 in 71 men (1.4%) in the United States have been raped at some time in their lives, including completed forced penetration, attempted forced penetration, or alcohol/drug facilitated completed penetration. (2)

- More than half (51.1%) of female victims of rape reported being raped by an intimate partner and 40.8% by an acquaintance; for male victims, more than half (52.4%) reported being raped by an acquaintance and 15.1% by a stranger. (2)

- An estimated 13% of women and 6% of men have experienced sexual coercion in their lifetime (i.e., unwanted sexual penetration after being pressured in a nonphysical way); and 27.2% of women and 11.7% of men have experienced unwanted sexual contact. (2)

- Most female victims of completed rape (79.6%) experienced their first rape before the age of 25; 42.2% experienced their first completed rape before the age of 18 years. (2)

- More than one-quarter of male victims of completed rape (27.8%) experienced their first rape when they were ten years of age or younger. (2)

"Please Stop the Insanity"

One of my biggest fights occurred throughout my youth. It swerved its way through the sexual abuse. It made its appearance many times through the physical abuse. And lastly became one of the biggest fights that I have every fault in my life. Welcome to the end of the beginning.

Scene 2

Judge, who me?

Domestic Violence is destroying the structure of families. It is killing the woman, destroying men and annihilating children all over this planet. It's like a disease spreading at rapid speed with no tendencies of slowing down. It's been moving like wildfire, destroying everything in its sight and with it taking no prisoners. Filled with rage, its core is wrapped around hate, disgust, manipulation and mainly control. In general, it has no preference and shows itself within men and women. Statistics show that more men commit this act of violence than women. But we do know that women are becoming angrier and therefore find themselves on the other end of committing the violence as well. Because of the belief in society, I don't necessarily see it slowing down anytime soon. In society people still, struggle with ownership and the belief that a woman is a man's property to do with as he pleases. So because of that, it's hard to see statistics going down but this will only continue to cause me to fight harder for this social injustice.

For years I worked with domestic violence and sexually abused survivors as a therapist. Many of them felt defeated by society because they felt unheard and blamed. Society has a hard time recognizing and understanding why women stay and therefore the survivor is blamed for allowing it to happen, which is what society expresses. In this world, we don't understand all of the dynamics that are involved when a person is abused so we have to become more educated so that we can support those that we know are in this type of relationship. It's our duty as we fight for human rights.

Also many times we are a part of a system that only sees physical abuse worthy of immediate concern, and even proving this at times can be a struggle, especially if the abuser is very manipulative. Our system is slowly catching up with the effects of psychological, verbal and emotional abuse and how it affects those that are exploited. There is such a huge need for education around domestic violence and we should all be a part of this crusade. This is a human rights issue in which all should be involved. Woman and children are dying every day due to one person wanting control over the other. When is this going to stop?

Since the prehistoric day's society has also shown that women are the property of a man. Women are treated as if they are only here to fulfill men's desires. There is truth behind the often hidden belief that men have the right to treat their mate anyway that they please, due to the assumption that women are their property. So thinking with that mentally makes it easy for men to see women as objects. And if you see a woman as an object, for example, a trashcan then it really wouldn't bother them to kick her or to punch her because of objectivity. Many times a person doesn't care about an object because it has no life. It doesn't bleed, it doesn't talk back, and it's just there to do what it was made to do.

Woman – Object – Beat- Property

There is a documentary that is comprised of all men discussing their views on domestic violence. As I watched this documentary I was amazed by their reaction to some of the questions asked. Ninety-nine percent of the men on the tape agreed that if they saw a woman with their mate walking down the street together and he slapped her in the face they would not jump in to protect her. Some of the individuals stated that the woman must have done something to make the man slap her, therefore the abuse was justified. Their overall thought process was that men in relationships had a right to control their mate in any way possible. I found it interesting that when asked the question about if they saw a woman walking down the street by herself and a man just walked up to her and slapped her across the face, just about every one of them would have jumped in to protect her. "So what's the difference, is the question I ask today? Are we still so closed-minded in believing that women are still considered to be a man's property? For our world to change, we must change our minds and our thoughts. We must consider the rights of all human beings. A specific gender should not dictate a specific level of respect given to an individual.

With that said, here is my story in black and white. Take from it what you need and either help yourself or help someone in desperate need of protection and support.

What was it about me? What was it about me? What was it about me that could never seem to be right or to get it right? What was it about me that would make a man think that he could take advantage of me? What was it about me that would make a man think that he could abuse me? What was it about me that would make someone hate me without even knowing who I was? What was it about me that would ask God to take my life? What was it about me? What was it about me that would make me doubt myself? God, I ask you, what was it about me that made me so gullible, naïve, and just plain old stupid? Yes, I said it, "Stupid", because that's how I felt.

Was it the way that I talked? Was it the way that I walked? Was it the way that I ran from life's problems? Was it the way that I smiled or could it had been the way that my eyebrows came together when I got angry? Could it have been the thoughts in my head that sometimes wished that I was no longer here living on earth? Could it have been that loud, awful scream that I made when the pain became too much to bear? What was it? Could it have been that I was just me? Was being me so bad? Really! Many people wonder what their purpose is in life. We wonder if we would be the next best thing. We usually have a vision of greatness and being on top of the world. But never in a million years did I think that my life would have taken the routes in which it has taken. This ride has been full of twists and turns lined with emptiness and self-destruction. Self-destruction and pity. Pity and misery. Misery and more misery. It was what I considered to be hell.

So living self destructively became a part of who I was lurking to see how I could ruin the rest of my life. I feel like there was a piece of me that was seeing how far I could go to ruin my life since everyone else had taken part in doing that as well. I didn't want for everyone else to have all the fun of destroying who I was, so I took what I thought was a piece of my control back. Disillusioned right? I know! But when you feel as though emptiness exudes every fiber of your being, making you feel like it was not just emptiness that you felt but that you was emptiness, you believe things to be true when they weren't. Can you imagine what it would be like to be Emptiness? Such a dreadful state of being, but that's where I lived. I lived in Emptiness. I was Emptiness! Emptiness is the state of containing nothing. And if I say that I was emptiness, I was in a state of containing nothing inside of me and that's how the world treated me. They treated me like nothing. It was a representation of something so removed and farfetched for many but within my presence on a daily basis. That inner child within me constantly fought against myself but I had nothing to fight with because I was empty.

My distorted thought process began at such a young age that it scared me and eventually grew to become my identity as I got older. I was always consumed with fear and could never figure out why. By my late teens this distorted identity of who I was convoluted everything that was factual to me. And when things are convoluted it makes it difficult to think and function properly. It makes you question everything around you and therefore never leaving you with a sense of stability in your mind.

And when the mindset gets distorted not much can be done to alter it until that person afflicted can begin to unravel the mess that is in their head. And then and only then can change of one's distorted thoughts allow for an individual to recognize their potential and value to themselves.

Here is the beginning picture of who I thought I was and how I was perceived in life by others along with how I perceived myself. See when we can't believe in who we are, we take on the perception of what the world says we are and therefore this becomes us. When we allow for that to happen, we are now what everyone says that we are and that is self-destructive all in itself. Now if that isn't convoluted, I don't know what is.

Daddy's Little Girl!

Many young girls define themselves based off of a father's connection to them. Depending on whether or not a father was in their life can have an effect on how a person see's them self. Father's play such an important role in their child's life. That development period within their young lives partly is shaped by the father. This is shown in every aspect of their growth process. And when that piece is missing it can bring about disruptions to that young person mind. It's like a missing link that can only be filled by a father.

When I think about my connection to my father, it has been one of the most profound experiences that I will cherish for the rest of my life. One of the most exhausting but rewarding relationships that I have ever had. Throughout my life, I have sought in others the same type of love and respect but struggled to find it. A father's love is something that can never be broken or replicated. There is something magical about a father and his little girl. That bond is unbreakable!

Throughout my young life, there were times where I felt like I had to protect my father. The family didn't always have the nicest things to say about my dad. I would get very defensive and many times ran away crying because I never appreciated when they would make him out to be a bad guy. I would always try my best to defend the man that I loved. See to me my father could do no wrong and he stood 10 feet tall in my eyes but in reality, he's about 5'2' but stands with a heart as tall as the highest mountain. No one could ever speak harshly nor condemn my father in any way. As a child, he was and still is everything to me. Regardless of how much I was hurt emotionally by my father in his period of absence, it did not change my perception of who he was then nor now.

Picture it, the year was 1976, I was four years old when my father left my life for a moment. I still can remember it like it was yesterday. I was watching from my parent's bedroom window trying to sneak a peek at what was going on. I tried my best not be noticed by anyone. I was supposed to be in my bedroom but I could feel the tension in the air between my parents so I needed to see firsthand what was going on. While I was looking out the window my heart was crushed. I can remember watching my dad packing up his bags in the trunk of the car. I was so heartbroken. Watching this take place shattered me to my core. Just earlier that day my dad and I were relaxing on the sofa, eating a snack together. We were laughing and watching television. I thought that I was living in the perfect home. Everything seemed like a fairytale but come to find out, I was wrong. My parents were not happy together and their separation caused me and my father's separation which devastated me.

As a child, you don't fully understand the relationship between a man and a woman. All I knew was that my father was leaving and I couldn't figure out why. I began to question what I did wrong. I began to believe in my mind that if I could have done something differently, this situation would have never happened. Within my mind, I truly believed that maybe if I listened more to my parents or maybe if I was just a little quieter, or maybe? All of these questions began to run through my mind hoping to find the answer that would allow him to come back home. I sat many days and nights in my window waiting for my father to walk back through those doors but he never did. I would yearn for my father's love so much it would make me sick not to have him near me. I thought that he no longer loved me because he left. What could I have done so bad to make him want to leave me? He left me! Was I that bad? The thoughts in my minds lead me to believe that I was that bad. So, therefore, something happened to me that day. I became that lost child. Watching my father having to pack up his bags into the trunk of the car was the first devastating event that had ever happen to me and therefore made a lasting impression in my mind. I can remember tears pouring down my face profusely, my heart was beating non-stop and thinking to myself that life was over as I knew it. I believe that this traumatic event set me up in many ways for bad relationships to come.

About a year later, I remembered my father returning back into my life again. One of my favorite places to visit was my grandmother house. She made me feel special. So when mommy stated that we were going to visit Nanny I got excited. At the time I was not aware of my father staying with my grandmother on State Street in Camden NJ. So imagine my surprise what I saw as we got to her house. As we pulled up I saw someone sitting on the step. When I got out of the car and walked up the stairs towards the front door. I didn't recognize the man in front of me. It was a year since I have seen my father and he looked different. He had a lot of gray hair that was covering his whole head and face. When he saw me he had the biggest smile and so did I and we hugged for a long time. Neither one of us wanted to let the other go. Even though his appearance changed, the man I once cried out for one year ago did not. It was as if I had won the lottery at five years old. One of the best gifts a girl could ever receive. The gift of her father returning for good. After our reunion, I knew in my heart that he would never leave me again and I was right. When my dad made a promise to me, he kept them and he promised never to leave me again. He kept his word.

At that moment I made up in my mind that I would do everything in my power to make my father pleased with me so that he would never leave me again. My focus was on being the best daughter that I could be, perfect in his sight so that he would never have a reason to want to go. It took years for me to realize that the reason he left had nothing to do with me. So I carried that weight of believing that it was my fought at the age of 5 to keep my father around. I feared to lose him again and I was going to do whatever it took to make sure that this did not happen.

Love of a Man

We seek for many things in life. Speaking from the perspective of a woman many times we seek for things that are destructive to our whole self. One of the many things that we seek out for when were broken is for someone to come along and make us whole. Very destructive thinking on our part. Because what that tends to do is keep us bound by that person because we are looking for them to complete us and not looking within ourselves to do the work.

So for many years of my life, the only thing that I ever sought for continuously was the love of a man. Within my heart was a hole that could only be filled by a man. That desire, that yearning, that necessity to have him no matter how he existed in my life was constant. And when he came into my life there was something about me that felt the need to protect him. In my desperate need to have a connection with someone, it led me to accept treatment that was unhealthy. I found myself trying to seek man's approval. No matter what the man was about, as long as he was there physically in my presence, it didn't matter what he did to me or didn't do for me. Keeping the peace and being the fixer was a part of who I was at that time, a trait I later hated.

What a huge character flaw that was to have. It was something that I learned from childhood, wanting to fix everything so that my father would stay. I never wanted to experience that type of pain again that I felt in missing my dad. Having another man walk out on me again would have been devastating. So in keeping what I thought was the love of man whether I was right or wrong, I felt as though that my job was to fix any and all situations.

I had to make sure that the man in my life was satisfied with the outcomes, regardless of my emotional state. It did not matter if I felt like less of a person. It did not matter if I was depressed. It did not matter if I felt suicidal because of the pain and torture that I endured on a daily basis. All that mattered was that he did not leave. I could deal with the rest.

For me, there was one big factor that continued to get in the way and that was the feeling of Loneliness! That feeling of loneliness can kill you if you let it. That thing called loneliness allowed me to deal with an individual that cared nothing about me. His only objective was to dominate and control my every thought, my every step, and my every emotion. When you're stuck in this state you don't have a mind of your own because you allow someone else to be in control of it. Loneliness is another type of fear which can set you so far back that you began to doubt yourself and God. It will have you doing things that would make you degrade yourself. At one point in my life, it made me accept all kinds of madness that the average person would not have accepted. It put me in a state of not believing that I was worth more than what I was telling myself. Being led to doubt my values as a human being, an individual and as a woman.

That feeling of loneliness which I feared for so many years led me to stay in an abusive relationship. A relationship that started out of fear and manipulation. A relationship that consisted of verbal, emotional and physical abuse for more than five years of my life. A relationship that had no boundaries. A relationship that uncovered years of desperation and heartache.

A relationship that was solely based on control. Sometimes when I look back on that relationship I have a hard time believing that I stayed and never fought back. Who was that girl that took all that abuse? Why did she stay? Why did she stay? The yearning for the love of a man is why I stayed.

When looking for the love of a man and loneliness is in place, it can make you feel passive and appear weak. When looking for the love of a man and you are insecure you tend to compromise your integrity. When looking for the love of a man and you doubt yourself you tend to accept whatever is in front of you. Ultimately, when looking for the love of a man while you are in a state of desperation it could lead to death.

Fact:
(Statistics was taken on February 13, 2015)
From the Center for Disease Control and Prevention
18,000
The Number of Women who have been killed by men in domestic violence disputes since 2003.

The Clouds

Let's begin! It was the beginning of the end. June of 1993. I wish that I could have foreseen the future because maybe I would have had a chance but then again maybe not. It was a very low time in my life. I was expelled from Delaware State College due to my inability to focus. During that last year of school, I was oblivious to what was going on around me. If I had to be honest with myself I barely attended class and the majority of my time was focused on drinking and getting high. There was a lot of uncertainty about my life goals, dreams, and aspirations. I had no interest in the law which was my major. Someone close to me thought that I would make a great lawyer due to being a great talker and this would be the perfect career for me. But I wanted to aspire to be an Architect but that dream got shot down. Because I was not great at math I was told that being an Architect was not the direction I should go. So I listen to their doubts about my abilities and in turn internalized them and made my decision based off of that. I don't regret much in life but that is one regret that I have because I love the structures of building and their unique designs. Anyway, that's not important right now, so back to the story at hand.

So at the time, my parents knew nothing about my status in school. I tried to cover it up by attending community college, hoping to raise my G.P.A to return to school in September. This lie never went forth the way in which I planned for it to go. While at school I met this man who seemed like a nice person. And for the sake of not revealing his name, I am choosing to call him Todd.

This book is not about revealing the batterer but it is about the victims, survivors that are seeking ways of making it through or who have made it through to the other side and this is in celebration of them. So please understand my reasoning for staying clear of revealing the batter's name. So anyway we know that people are always pleasant in the beginning and then they begin to show their true selves after some time. In the case of Todd, his craziness came out in our 3rd encounter. I should have heeded the blaring warning signs that something was not quite right with him. The signs were there and very obvious but I ignored them because I was lonely and obviously depressed.

As we began to get to know one another I found out more about him that I rather not have known. During our brief interactions together I would feel very nervous because of the things he would say. One day we were having a conversation where he expressed language that resembled someone that could be deemed as a stalker which should have deterred me but it didn't. He began talking about how he has been watching me for a while from afar. He then goes on to say that one of the things that he noticed was the fact that I never purchased lunch nor did I bring lunch whenever I came into the student center. I was a broke college student who couldn't afford to purchase anything to eat. Unemployed and therefore it was my responsibility to bring something from home.

Anyhow, on this particular day, Todd decided to purchase lunch for me. Earlier that day I had already made plans to get some homework done at the library Crazy enough I truly believed in my mind that if I worked hard during this summer semester that they would accept me back at Delaware State, so I worked hard in hopes of that happening. The library consumed much of my time that day so there was no extra time to go into the student center. By this time I had no clue that he was going to bring me lunch. We never had any previous conversation regarding spending lunch time together, so as usual, I did my own thing.

As the day was ending I headed toward the bus stop to go home and as I was approaching the area I saw someone running across the field. At first, I did not recognize the person, so I continued to walk but I did slow down my pace. A few seconds later I heard someone calling my name as they got closer to the area. When I recognized that it was him I stopped to see what was going on. Once he got close to me I noticed an angry look on his face. As he stared at me he started to raise his voice, questioning my whereabouts. While yelling at me he stated that he brought me lunch today and I was not where I was supposed to be, according to him. My first reaction was to begin laughing. He was acting like a raging fool in the middle of the parking lot. After a few moments of being yelled at my laughter turned into fear and nervousness. My eyes began to get very big because of his anger towards me and he would not stop yelling. I thought that this man was joking, but come to find out this was not a joking manner.

As I stood there watching him in action he continued to yell at me about my whereabouts and not being where he thought I should be. This statement alone made me skeptical about him. There is something wrong with someone that watches a person's every move to the point of getting upset if something changes within that person's day. He then stared at me, which seemed like a lifetime and without blinking his eyes, he said to me, "Don't you ever do that to me again," in an aggressive tone of voice and his finger pointing towards me. He was upset that he had just wasted his money on me and expressed in a bold tone that this better not happen again. He was talking to me as if I was his child. As I mentioned earlier, this all happened only after our 3rd encounter and we had only seen each other on the college campus. I tried covering up my feelings by laughing, but I was extremely embarrassed and had never been placed in this type of situation before. After his explosion and when he calmed down, I asked him if he still had the food that he purchased. He said yes and showed me the bag. So I asked him if I could have it. As he handed me the bag, he made it very clear that the next time he better not have to look for me or else. He said this in a stern, low voice, close to my ear. After hearing that, I did not respond to him in any way. As we walked and got on the bus, I began to eat my food and proceeded as if nothing ever happened.

While I was riding the bus, I could remember thinking to myself: here is a man that looks ok and is paying some attention to me. Even though I thought in my head that he might be a little crazy, it felt flattering that someone felt the need to do something kind for me. I began thinking, if only I could have been in the student center, as usual, this would have never occurred and we would have been on our way to a great start. At least that's what I convinced myself to believe. His kindness and the way in which he was looking out for me was appealing. What I thought to be an act of kindness, ended up being an act of craziness. From the time we got on the bus until I was dropped off, he was very clingy, as if we were already in a relationship. He didn't say much to me on the ride home but continued to give me these looks in which I couldn't figure out what he was thinking. He was very intimidating.

I had been yearning to receive attention because of the way in which I felt about myself, and Todd provided what I needed at the time. I held on to it for dear life. As I stated earlier I felt like I was loneliness waiting for someone to come along. And when you are crying out for wholeness many times as myself, we accept the first thing that comes along. Attention was attention no matter what it looked like for me. Regardless of the type of attention I got, he still gave me what I thought I needed, whether good or bad.

Let me tell you about how seeking attention can destroy a person. When where a child we seek for the love and attention of our parents. That connection we feel towards our parents is formed at birth, therefore it's a feeling that many of us as children don't want to relinquish. Sometimes it plays out when there are other siblings in the home and that child is fighting for the attention of their parents. If that child perceives that the other child is receiving more attention, then that child could grow up feeling neglected and in turn began to seek outside which can bring negative attention. As we grow and get into our teen years we sometimes seek attention from our peers and those around us, due to the lack of perceived attention at home and many times if we are not careful that attention turns into developing bad habits such as using drugs, becoming sexually active and doing things that are unhealthy. And lastly, as that adult, we tend to seek even more negative attention that can be destructive to our lives.

The Ride

Todd was very interesting. He never asked me to be his girlfriend but the relationship between the two of us just thrived very quickly into something I never expected. After being expelled from College and breaking up with my college boyfriend due to the distance, I was not interested in being with anyone else. But once again Todd made me feel wanted. He began calling me regularly. It was flattering to have a man pay attention to me but it was also scary because he was possessive. Even though his constant calling was a little ridiculous it helped me to refocus my attention. Our relationship unraveled quickly. Too quickly some would say because we never took the time to get to know one another. We barely knew anything about each other but it did not stop us from sleeping with one another which caused a whole lot of trouble quickly for us.

Most of the time abuse usually begins very early and sometimes it doesn't start with a fist in your face, therefore, victims sometimes have a hard time recognizing it. I want to talk about what jealousy and possessiveness look like and how it can destroy a relationship. As I mentioned earlier I was a broke college student and every day I would have to catch the bus and normally I would catch it at the same time. When you become a regular passenger many times the bus drivers are the same so they get to know your face. This one particular driver I will call Dave was very friendly and he and I would have conversations to pass the time along while I rode to school. Dave would talk about his wife and family events that would occur throughout his day, and I would share the same type of information as well. Our conversation was strictly platonic with no underlying meaning.

One day I was late for school and I had to catch a different bus than normal. Due to our classes being held at the same time Todd and I rode on the same bus together. On this particular day, he managed to make it to school on time, which in turn sparked up a conversation between him and Dave, the bus driver. Dave knew that Todd and I sat together every day so he felt comfortable asking Todd was I alright because I wasn't at the bus stop as normal. I found all of this out when I finally arrived at school that day by Todd.

After class, I went to the student center as usual, and I saw that Todd was there. As I began to walk towards him to say hi, the look on his face was threatening. Before I could say good morning to him, he began to read me the riot act in the middle of the student center. He wanted to know why the bus driver was asking questions about me. He then began accusing me of sleeping with him. He was very irritated and I couldn't understand why this was happening. Todd continued to ramble off question after question out of his mouth in regards to Dave and me. I wanted to respond, but he continued to yell stating that the bus driver better not ever ask him another question again about me or else. "Or else what?" I responded. At that moment I watched him bite his lip as he worked hard not to say anything else regarding the subject. He never did respond. I then looked at him, very puzzled, and began to laugh hysterically. This whole situation was stupid, though funny to me. I barely knew this man and already he was acting like some jealous fool. He was not even considered "my man" to begin with and had no right to act this way. Deep down inside a part of me was flattered about his reaction, as crazy as it may seem.

The common sense part of me knew that something was wrong with this situation and the best thing for me at that time would have been to run away quickly. So, why didn't I run away? Well, having this craziness around, pushed those feelings of loneliness out the window and won over my common sense.

Sometimes I think back and I wonder why I didn't listen to those thoughts in my head. There were warning signs of even more potentially dangerous situations occurring, but I did not take heed to them. I did not feel confident about myself, therefore, I allowed someone else to have control over what I thought about me. Todd's attention made me feel special therefore I believed that if only I would have listened to him or been at the proper place, he would have never gotten so angry. I realize now that because I lacked that ultimate feeling of loving myself, he took advantage of what was in front of him. There was a part of me that believed that he was the only one that would care about me so I did not want to walk away from that. And I knew that it was an irrational thought that didn't make any sense but when you lose sight of reality irrational tends to be rational.

Jealously! Such an interesting word that holds so many people stuck. There is a belief that there is such a thing as healthy jealousy. It could look pretty innocent and loving to the one that's on the other side receiving those feelings of jealousy. By the way, what does it mean to be jealous? Having feelings or showing some suspicion of someone's unfaithfulness in a relationship. So can this be healthy? I don't know! I guess it all depends on the circumstances. Because if I have a suspicion that my spouse is unfaithful and their not, that can truly cause an issue to occur. That person begins to get so suspicious of their spouse every move that it can become aggressive whether verbally or physically all because of suspicion, which is not factual. Jealousy can be so dangerous in a relationship and people need to be careful when coming across someone that shows these tendencies. No one wants to be blamed for someone's imagination.

So what is the bottom line behind jealously? I truly believe that having low self-esteem is at the core of a jealous person. And that's because when a person thinks less of themselves they have to put that off on someone else and therefore it hides their flaws within themselves. It's a masking and protection for that individual who is very unhealthy. And ultimately if the jealous individual does not work on themselves, their actions can begin to show behaviors of possessiveness towards their spouse, which is taking the jealousy to another level.

In regards to the victims experiencing this behavior towards them, many times they take the jealousy as a form of love. But what is that false love about? Honestly, for me, it was about those feelings of being desired when I felt so undesirable. There was something missing that needed to feel wanted so when he behaved in a jealous manner I felt whole. He paid attention. Who cares that it was negative attention?

We must care about us even if no one else cares. That's how we protect ourselves from being someone else's possession.

Destroyed

As I watched others in relationships, admiring their courtship, I wondered why I hadn't experienced that yet. Time was spent getting to know one another and therefore eventually an, "Ask" was given and she accepted. Up to this point, I had never experienced getting to know a person in this way. For some reason for me, it just happened. So I think about how did this relationship with Todd just happen? Did he ever ask me to be his girlfriend? No, I don't think so. Did we even communicate our emotions and feelings towards one another? No, I don't think so. Did we even really look at each other as if we were attracted to one another? No, I don't think so. So how did we even get to a place of a relationship? There was never a moment of deciding whether or not we were going to date. It just happened.

So when things just happen, that leaves you wide open for anything a person brings to the table. I would think about why Todd even wanted to be bothered with me. According to him, I was not his type of female. Nothing I ever did please him. He criticized many things that I did or tried to do. There was no encouragement from him to me, no real words that expressed love and compassion. I could never seem to do anything right in his eyes. I felt like he was looking for someone to control and he hit the jackpot when he found me. Todd had a tendency of always comparing me to the women in his culture. He would insinuate that Black American women were not good enough for him. No matter what I did, I could never be what he wanted me to be.

And honestly, I can understand where he got this thinking from because when I was in his home where his mother and stepfather lived there was a constant conversation about how stupid black American women were and how we were less intelligent.

And this type of conversation was held right in front of me as if I wasn't even there. And that's how Todd treated me like I wasn't even there.

More days than not, I thought about why was I even entertaining the thought of being with a man like this? It was heartbreaking to be knocked down and belittled almost every day. And the thing about it was that we held no interest in one another. We didn't like the same things. We didn't listen to the same music, and we didn't enjoy the same foods. We had one connection and one connection only and sad to say, that was sex. That all! We were physically attracted to each other, but outside of the bed, there was nothing.

A word to the wise! If a person doesn't love you for who you are, there is absolutely nothing that you can do to make them accept you. Never allow any man or woman make you feel like less of a person due to their insecurities. Don't give them that authority over your life, like I did.

As I mentioned earlier, our relationship was based on sex. Before we even knew each other's last name, sex became a major part of us being together. Sex distorted and covered up the truth. He had no respect for me and I had no respect for myself. He wanted sex on the bus, in the woods, in the car and whatever he wanted he got it, no matter how it made me feel. I was nothing to him. But if only I would have taken the time to get to know him then maybe I could have seen who he was and not fallen so hard. I didn't know this man at all. I found myself sleeping with the enemy.

One of the biggest things that an abuser will do is work to pull their spouse away from their friends and family, which is intentionally done. The batterer does this with the hopes of removing her or him from any means of support. Todd worked hard to destroy my long-time relationships with many of my friends. He wasted no time seeking to destroy relationships that I had with people that were in my life way before he came along. Part of the issue was that I did not recognize what he was doing from the start. How he strategically set out to remove those important people out of my life. One by one people were drifting further and further away from me and I couldn't understand why. My circle of friends was always filled with many loved ones. Some were true to me and others were acquaintances, but they all served a purpose in my life. He tore that apart completely. And if my eyes were open at the time, I would have noticed how his life was opposite of mine in that he did not have friends that he was close too. I can remember one friend and even he was not around a lot. I never took notice of how he excluded himself from the world. He wanted me to be just like him.

One evening I had invited some of my girlfriends over to the house. I was still living with my mom in which she was very open to having guest over. They were home from college for summer break. These three friends of mine were very close to me and close to my heart. We always had a good time together laughing and joking with one another. When we got together we would reminisce about our college experience together. Getting drunk together, getting high together, and getting into fights with other groups of people together. Well ok, it might not sound like fun to you but we had an awesome time finding out who we were as young adults and we did it together.

So I was looking forward to their visit. I knew that they would cheer me up because what they didn't know was that I was feeling depressed and lonely. Every time I would speak to them over the phone I would sound upbeat and happy but I knew how to mask my pain. I did it for most of my life. I needed to see them to help me feel alive again and be a part of something or someone. So when they got to the house we all laughed and were excited like little girls and we were having a great time sitting in the living room being amongst one another.

After some time without notice, Todd decided to come past the house. He knew that I was having friends over from college because I told him earlier, but obviously, that did not matter. He wanted his hair braided and apparently, he couldn't wait for my company to leave. At first, I stated to him that I could do his hair later when my friends left, but in Todd's fashion he looked at me and stated in a stern voice that he wanted his hair done now. He did not care that I was enjoying myself and as a matter of fact, it was an issue that I was enjoying myself with someone else other than him. He placed no importance on what mattered to me. So as we sat down for me to do his hair, one of my girlfriends looked at me with a look of concern. I looked back at her and shook my head and nothing was ever mentioned about it.

As the girls and I continued to have a good time together even though I was still braiding his hair, I received a phone call from one of my close male friend's from college. He was an ex-boyfriend but we stayed in touch. His call was unexpected but appreciated, therefore, I was so excited to hear from him. I knew that I couldn't talk long because I had company, so we talked for a brief moment.

As I was going to explain to him that I had company and that I would call him later, in front of everyone Todd snatched the phone out of my hand and hung it up while my friend was still on the phone. At that moment my heart was beating very fast. I didn't know what to say or to do at that moment. Todd had a look on his face that was scary and full of anger. So in front of my company, he dared me to pick up the phone and call my friend back. I was extremely embarrassed. It felt as though I was having an out of body experience. I had no clue about what to say or what to do. I tried to crack a joke so that I would not crumble inside. I started laughing at what just happened and I tried to play it off as if he was joking. Laughing was the only way for me to deal with this. It was my defense mechanism. What I noticed was that my girlfriends also started to laugh saying that Todd was crazy in a humorous way but I knew that this was much more serious. I knew I was going to have to deal with the consequences later that evening. After sitting there for a few minutes, I decided to get up out of my chair and proceeded to walk towards the kitchen. As I made my way there, I heard his footsteps behind me. As I reached the kitchen I stopped in the middle of the floor and looked at him. Then I commenced to try and talk to him in a low tone so that no one else could hear us but that didn't work too well. I asked Todd why he embarrassed me in that way and his only response was that I was not allowed to speak to another guy under no circumstances. He demanded that my time is spent with him and him only. I was surprised by the way in which he reacted. He knew that I had people in my life that loved and supported me but that did not matter to him. When he and I came back into the living room my friends decided to leave and from this point on our friendships was never the same. For some time I couldn't understand why they disconnected from me. Were they able to see what I saw in him? That was a defining moment in how I lost many of the connections with the world. He was very adamant about it being only the two of us. I had never experienced anything like this before. I was 20 years of age, and unsure of what was love and what was control. I didn't understand it nor did I have the safety to talk to anyone about it. His anger, his rage, his deceit, his control. And needless to say, I never returned the call of my friend and we did not reconnect until 22 years later when he found me on social media.

Power & Control! Power & Control are the ultimate pieces of an abusive relationship. The batterer is seeking to have control over his or her victim. And control is what Todd wanted over my life. Control over me gave him strength and power within himself. The power that he lacked. His personal life was filled with pain and loneliness. Todd expressed on many occasions of having low self-esteem and not being able to love himself due to his past. He was filled with anger and resentment towards his mother and father and therefore had anger and resentment towards everyone that came into contact with him. I didn't realize I was just another pawn in his game. He never liked the fact that I had friends and family that loved me. Something that he never experienced. His motive was to ultimately tear me away from every one of them if he could. With some people, he won that battle of breaking us apart and with others, we constantly fought because I continued to be in my family's life no matter what he tried to do. I just dealt with the consequences at a later time.

There is never a timetable to when and how abuse begins within a relationship. Sometimes it can be a gradual process and other times it can happen from the very start. Either way it a scary thing to experience because it always comes at an unexpected time. A time where the confusion arises because one minute they are saying, I love you and the next minute they are calling you stupid. How can these both happen within the same conversation? Well, they do and many victims get confused about what to believe and what not to believe.

Well, Todd and I became enmeshed with each other from the very beginning. Most of our days were spent going to class and when we were not in class we were smoking weed together. Smoking marijuana was a behavior that I continued since the age of 12, but that's a story for another time. As I mentioned before, sex was a core part of our relationship. Truthfully that's all that it was and therefore three months into the relationship I became pregnant. I had a lot of fear regarding whether or not I wanted to carry this man's baby. Doing so would keep me attached to him for the rest of my life. Over a few weeks of discussing the pregnancy and how we both felt about going through with it, we both came to the conclusion that we were going to have a child together. His conversation regarding the pregnancy was neither pleasant nor uplifting but more threatening. He often told me what I was going to do and how I was going to do it. So even if I wanted a say in the matter, I felt like I did not have a say regarding my life.

So here I was pregnant, with no education, unemployed, living with my mother, and depressed. At this point in my life I had no direction, nor did I have any idea of what I wanted to do. I had three years of college and nothing to show for it.

I was a failure, not having any specific direction in life. And the worst part about it was that I was in a relationship that was meaningless and abusive. A relationship that expressed no love, and no concern for others. How did I know what a relationship was supposed to entail? My relationship in college was loving but short due to him graduating and moving back home. I felt alone and felt the need to be with someone so I held on and stayed with Todd through the Dr. Jekyll and Mr. Hyde performances.

I can reminder it like it was yesterday, the very first time he became physically abusive. Believe me when I tell you that it took me totally by surprise. I had gotten used to being called names and threatened about different situations of what I should and should not do, but up to this point, he had never put his hands on me. Let me set the scene for you: It was around 10 o'clock in the morning and no one else was home. The summer session at college was over and I was looking for a job. On this one particular morning, I was not expecting him to show up at the house without notice. I was still in my flannel nightgown when he came. From the beginning, he was never one to compliment me. When he came to the house it was always about him and what I could do for him. This particular morning I remember not feeling well physically. While pregnant I would get sick a lot with morning sickness, afternoon sickness, and evening sickness. It didn't matter. I was always hungry and consumed with heartburn. After some time of him being at the house and without warning, he began yelling at the top of his lungs, making demands and belittling my character. He wanted me to cook for him at that very moment but I didn't feel well and he couldn't understand that.

So in turn, I began to yell and scream at the top of my lungs back at him. He hated when I would stand up for myself. I guess he expected me to bow down to him and take what he gave and in the beginning, I did not, therefore, this led to even more abuse. Todd began to speak out of his mouth obscenities of all kinds, including words that were used for female dogs. He termed me as being worthless. After his words were not enough and he saw that I was not being affected in the way that he would have liked, he began to walk towards me with an expression of anger. I was conscious of his every step and as he got closer I would back away. Next thing you know Todd pushed me into the wall. As my head hit the wall he reached out his arms and grabbed me by my neck, throwing me like a rag doll back and forth. My head continuously pounded up against the wall which seemed like a lifetime. I thought that I was going to lose the baby because of the constant way in which he was throwing me back and forth. I can remember grabbing my head as it was hitting the wall and crying profusely. I began to feel lightheaded after a while and disoriented. My breathing was shallow because he had such a hard grip on my neck. I was hoping that something within him would feel some compassion that would make him stop. I tried my best to escape from him, but it wasn't easy. He did eventually let go of my neck, only to grab me by my nightgown and snatched off all of the buttons. I remembered screaming and trying to push him away, hoping he would leave but nothing changed. Within minutes, he left me alone and began to pace around the living room like a madman. He was yelling, why do you make me do these things to you? Blaming me for his actions. His hands were flying around in the air and he was unstable at that point. While this was going on I was standing in the dining room. I began to gaze off and noticed that there were blinking lights outside of my house. Apparently, he must have seen them as well because a few minutes later he then took a look outside and saw that the police were sitting in between my home and the neighbor's home. I was praying that they were called to help me, but they never came and knocked on the door. I just stood there with my nightgown ripped open, in fear, hoping and wishing that someone would come to my rescue. When he looked out the window for a minute he got himself together quickly, looked over in my direction and left the house. For a while, I began to pace the floors of the living room wondering what to do. Nothing like this had ever happened to me before. I was confused, scared, and nervous, along with many other feeling all at once. I never said anything to anyone regarding what happen. I remember being afraid to leave him because I was pregnant and I did not want to be alone raising our child.

Never would I have believed that Todd would have harmed me in this way. My head and my neck was in so much pain. I had no clue why he treated me this way. At that very moment was when I started to blame myself for everything that happened in that relationship. I truly believed that if I had only kept my mouth shut in the beginning, it would have never gotten this far. I was so angry at myself. Why did I assert myself? What made me think that he would respond positively to my yelling? He never did before, so what made me think that this time would have been different? So it made it easier to blame me and to forgive him. Later on that evening he called to apologize and promised never to hurt me or the baby again. He repeatedly begged for my forgiveness. He begged me not to leave him. He begged me to give him another chance. He begged me not to tell anyone. He also promised me that he has never put his hands on a woman and he didn't know what came over him. So, of course, I didn't leave and for the remainder of our relationship, I don't know if I believed him that every time he apologized that it wouldn't happen again or if I was just too afraid to do anything about it and leave.

As the relationship progressed, the physical abuse grew more frequent. One evening there was a chase going on. I never realized that when I got into this relationship that I was going to have to learn how to run track just like him. One evening our daughter and I stayed the night with him at his mother's home. She and her husband was away for the weekend as usual, which is when many of the incidents occurred. In the beginning, everything seemed ok that day. We were watching television just relaxing. After a while, I began craving for a cigarette not realizing until then that I was all out. I wanted to go to the store but we didn't have the car keys. Earlier that day we were out with family riding in their car so we didn't need to carry around car keys that day. As I proceeded to look for the keys to the car I could not find them. So now the both of us began to look diligently for them but to no avail. In trying to trace our steps, he asked me to call my mom to see if the keys were at her house. It was pretty late when all of this was taking place so I felt like it was better to wait until the morning time to call her so that she wouldn't have to get up out of her sleep. Big mistake on my part! Since I couldn't go to the store I decided to take a shower and when I came out of the bathroom he had apparently called my mom and asked her to drop off the keys. I was upset that he had no regard for anyone but himself. It wasn't like we were stranded somewhere and needed a way home. We were safe in the house so in my mind it could have waited. I believe that he should have had enough respect and waited until the morning, but I kept my mouth shut and let it go. About a half an hour later, I decided to get dressed and go to the store as I had intended to do earlier. As I went to grab the keys to the car, he began yelling and cursing. He decided that since I did not obey his orders to call my mom, in the beginning, I had no right to touch the keys to his car. Just that quick it went from our car to his car. Anyway, he was yelling so loud that the baby began to cry as she was playing on the floor. Next thing I know he began to walk towards me looking very angry, so I began to move backward going around the back end of the table, near the patio door. It was a tight area so it was not easy to maneuver in that space. His movement towards me began to get faster and faster, to the point where he was chasing me back and forth around the table. After realizing that he was not going to stop chasing me, I quickly darted for the kitchen and found myself up against the wall with no place to go. That was the wrong thing to do. I left myself without any place to go. At that moment I saw him raise his right fist and as he swung it towards my head, I was able to duck just in time. His fist went straight through the kitchen wall and left a huge hole there, which is an indication of how hard he was swinging at my face. I felt the wind of the swing as I ducked down. While he was pulling his fist out of the wall I ran past him, scooped up my daughter out of the middle of the floor, and ran into one of the bedrooms. I quickly locked the door behind me and placed a chair under the door knob so that he could not get in. I wanted to go out of the front door, but because it would take too much time to find the house keys and unlock the door, I ran to the next safe place. One of the bedrooms were the only choice for safety. There was a window in the room that was in front of the house near the front door. I was planning to climb out of the window but he came to the front door to keep an eye on us preventing us from escaping. He was going back and forth between banging on the door, yelling to let him in, and going to the front door to make sure that we were not trying to leave. After some time he was getting tired. The banging stopped and he started to plead with me to come out. He promised not to harm me if I would just come out of the room. I was so afraid of him. I felt like as if he could have gotten so angry that he could have killed me. So I decided to stay in the room. I slept on the floor without any blankets with my baby wrapped up in my shirt until daybreak. When I woke up I was trying to decide whether to try to go out the window again or face him. I was hesitant to leave that room. I had no clue of his state of mind. I knew that our daughter needed to eat and I need to change her pamper but everything was in the living room. So I put my ear to the door to see if I could hear any movement and I then decided to walk out with caution and fear trembling through my body. As I proceeded out of the room he was cooking breakfast and extremely apologetic, begging me again not to leave him. Just about every time he would abuse me he would tell me about his past of being abused as a child for sympathy I guess. And somehow it would end up being about him and me consoling his emotions. Crazy making is what I call it! But once again I decided to stay since he was extremely apologetic. Our day continued as if nothing happen which was the norm.

When his parents returned home I was very nervous. I watched his mom as she walked into the kitchen. I saw her stare at the big hole in the wall. What I found interesting was that this was her home and she never expressed at that moment any concerns about what could have happened to the wall. Who would come into their home and find a big hole in the wall and not inquire about it? That made absolutely no sense to me. But it did make me wonder if Todd had already said something to her before she got home. She acted as if there was nothing there to question. Some time later she did say to me that if someone ever hit her she would leave them and she hopes that I would do the same. That was the only comment mentioned that could have referenced the reasoning for the hole in the wall. But she never confronted her son. I was hoping that she could make him accountable for his action. I was hoping that she could do what I feared to do but she didn't.

I was broken by this point. I thought that if Todd parents saw the hole in the wall that they would demand an answer and therefore demand him to change. Not that anyone could make another person change, but I was hoping for the best. I thought that help had arrived but it only got worse from there on. I felt like he knew that his parents knew what was going on and that they accepted his behavior, so he figured why would he change? I believed in this theory that I came up with because it made sense to me. Why else would it intensify? This man loved to tear me down verbally. There was never a passing day where he did not speak to me like I was an animal. I just got to the point where I didn't care about what he did or said to me. I began to expect it, and when it happened it was a normal part of my daily existence. Seeing as though it occurred so much, nothing that he did to me was a surprise anymore. Never in my life have I ever been called so many names that had nothing to do with love. Love is gentle, love is kind, love is patient, love understands. He had no concept of what love consisted of, and constantly used vulgar language towards me. His love for me did not fit any of those characteristics. This man had no clue about what love entailed. The words that he expressed to me about love were something to keep me, and it worked.

People are being beaten, battered and bruised every day and in the same breath are being told, "I love you". How could this be? How could a person that abuses another individual believe that the word love exists in a place of pain and horror? Why are love and the word abuse seen as being synonymous? If we truly understood what the word love means then we could understand that there is no connection. We have to be able to understand what love consists of and how it should portray its self to us as human beings.
Love is an unconditional feeling that removes selfishness from the equation and allows for the other person to receive the best of who we are.

And Abuse is the total opposite where selfishness plays the larger role. Abuse is hateful, evil, manipulative, deceitful, twisted, full of rage and wicked which is designed to bring a person down within themselves. Abuse doesn't care nor does it have any concern for others.

So we have to believe and understand that in looking at these two words when a person abuses us and says that they love us, the truth does not resonate with them. Therefore when you are on the other side receiving the abuse there is a sense of self-worth that must kick-in to escape. No one has a right to hurt us. No one! Not even in the name of LOVE.

It's amazing what happens to the mind when your life takes an alternate route. A route you never was sure about nor planned. But after seeing what life had given you sometimes it takes things like this to begin to see a future that you thought was gone. A future full of creativity and excitement. I can remember as a child always imagining. Bright colors were a huge theme in my mind. I would have thoughts of owning my own business even as young as five years old. I was an artist creating greeting cards with my artwork and selling them to family and friends in the neighborhood for twenty-five cents apiece. At the age of 12 years old, I learned how to bake cookies and started my own cookie business selling to the local entrepreneurs and I was in demand on a regular basis. So I tell you all of this so that you can understand that I had dreams. I had a purpose. I had desires as young as five years old and they were twisted and distorted as I got older.

While I was in this dysfunctional relationship with Todd, I began to think about going back to school and attending community college on a full-time basis. I knew that it would be harder now because it was no longer just me because I had a baby in my stomach. So unlike before I now had to work as well. I was employed working in a local department store making minimum wage to help support our child. But I knew that in order for me to do something different with my life that I was going to need an education. So when I decided to make that move, I brought this information to Todd's attention. We were at his mother's home when I decided to tell him about my plans for the future. I couldn't remember the last time I was this excited about something.

And I believe it was the first time that I felt like I had a purpose again. A feeling that I thought I lost. So I was hoping for the same type of excitement from him but when I told him he looked disappointed and not excepting. Why did I think anything different? Why did I think that he would respond positively to me seeking to be successful? His interest in me was to keep me down, not to keep me up. Anyway, Todd said to me that there was no need for me to continue school anymore because he had decided to go back to college and only one of us could do that. According to him, both of us could not attend school at the same time. Interestingly enough neither one of us was paying for our college education, so why would it matter if we both attended school at the same time. My mother was paying for my education and his mother was paying for his, so finances had nothing to do with whether or not we both attended school at the same time. Which led me further to understand that this had nothing to do with finances but all to do with control.

For him, it was all about control once again. If I graduated with my Bachelor's degree and gained a sense of self-worth then there could have been a possibility of me believing in myself and then eventually leaving this relationship. I believed that this scared him, therefore, he wanted to make all of the decisions for me. He wanted to rule on what I could do and what I couldn't do. And to make matters worse, when we had this conversation his mother was sitting at the table with us and she agreed with her son. She made it clear to me that my life was over due to being pregnant and my only focus should be on the child, not my education.

My responsibilities should now be on being a wife, which we weren't married and a mother and these should be my only goals in life, according to her. So after she said that, I watched them together discussing and planning my life and deciding for me what should be my focus.

A little while later they both agreed that I should at least wait until he was done with school before I even thought about continuing my college education. I felt so defeated and ganged up on at that moment. I remember going to the bathroom and crying because I felt lost and confused. But instead of doing what my heart told me to do, which was to leave and take my life in my hands, I listened to them and decided to wait on pursuing my education but only for a brief moment.

What I have learned through years of healing and gaining knowledge in the field of domestic violence is that keeping a person from furthering their education and advancing in life is another form of abuse. People who seek to control another human being are not looking for their spouse to grow and advance in life because then that person becomes a threat to their relationship and could support themselves. And if they can support themselves and become a stronger human being, than they will eventually remove themselves from the abusive situation. When a person feels intimidated by a spouse, it brings on a worthless feeling within one's self. No one should have the ability to dictate how a person grows and develops. As human beings, we have the ability to exceed far and wide beyond anyone's comprehension and can only be stagnated if we began to be controlled by another human being.

Being young and pregnant does not mean that a person's life is over. All it means is that you might have to push and work a little harder, but everything is still within your means to obtain. If you are reading this book and you feel like there are people stopping you from moving forward, please do whatever you have to do to take care of yourself. Even if it means walking around them, walking over them or walking through them to get away from them.

Never allow anyone to stop your progress in life. Never allow control from another human being to place a pause in your journey to healing nor your journey to success.

And that success can look like whatever you have deemed it to reflect. You have to take your thoughts, your fears and your questions to God and He will show you the plan and the way. No one else should have that compass to direct your path.

Honeymoon

With many things in life, we have a honeymoon period. In our jobs many times, in the beginning, there is that great honeymoon period where things are going so well and we are enjoying what we were hired to do. Everyone seems so nice and pleasant and then something happens. When we purchase new things we are in our honeymoon period where we are so excited about our new house or our new car. We are bragging to everyone about these things and then something happens and we began to despise those things that were once exciting to us. And then we fall in love and the honeymoon period is so amazing for many of us, but for some of us that honeymoon period never really existed, it was just a mirage.

Within domestic violence, there is something called the honeymoon stage and that is when in between the abuse there are moments of peace and what looks like kindness towards the victim. It's those moments where victims tend to see the man or woman that they once fell in love with and adored. The person that showed up as a kind and gentle soul. The person that was caring and compassionate so we thought. Many victims get stuck and the reason why many never leave. But also recognize that there are some victims that never receive rest and the honeymoon stage never shows up.

I was able to receive the benefits of rest from time to time and experiencing the honeymoon stage. I looked forward to them because I felt like maybe this day he will change and be different. Maybe this day he will recognize what he has done to me and gain a conscious. During one of our honeymoon stages, Todd decided to take our daughter and I out to dinner. Once in a while, we would do family things together and we would have fun with one another. So while at dinner the time that we spent together was very nice.

I tried to contain those negative thoughts that things were going to change for the worse but it was hard. I always knew in the back of my mind that this great feeling of euphoria was temporary. It was inevitable. But while things were pleasant and peaceful I enjoyed it. We talked, laughed and played with our daughter together. Quiet, pleasant and peaceful, those moments were very welcomed when they occurred. Toward the end of the dinner, I began to get anxious. I was wondering when he was going to change his skin. When was this nice guy in the world going to become himself? And what do you know, it took off right before my eyes.

We were about 5 minutes away from my house when he began to show his true self. It's as if a switch turned off and the world seemed different to him. As if he had just forgotten how we laughed together and played together. Was all of that an act and for the outside world to see? We did have people coming up to us stating how cute we all look together and how lucky I was to have a good man to take care of our daughter. Assumptions! Screwed Perceptions!

Anyway, as we were driving he began fussing at me about something that I did not do earlier that day. He truly believed that he was my boss and that he had authority over me and whatever he said should be the last word. Todd began to question me over and over again but I would not answer him. I refused to give him what he wanted. I was standing up for myself so I thought. But as his frustration began to build and his anger began to get heightened he started pressing on the gas pedal even harder, trying to intimidate me and place fear in me. But as all of this was going on, I just sat there quietly.

When I would not respond to his negative behavior, he then decided to press on the brakes extremely hard. Because of this, my chest hit the dashboard and my head hit the window. I began crying and screaming as I grabbed my head from the intense pain. He showed no reaction to what had just occurred. Then I turned to the back of the car to see if she was hurt and he pushed me back into my seat. Not caring about me or the baby, he began to drive again. While speeding, he reached over to my side of the car and tried to open the passenger door. His intentions were to throw me out of the car while it was moving. He kept screaming at the top of his lungs that he was going to kill me. I continued to push him away from me, screaming for him to stop. He was determined to throw me out of his car that night, but I held on tightly until we pulled up to my house. We continued to scream at each other until the baby and I were out of the car. Thankfully, while all of this was going on she was in her car seat showing no signs of physical damage. Before I removed myself from the car, I reached from the front seat to get my daughter out. I did not trust him. I was not getting out of his car before I pulled my daughter out first. He would have pulled off with her in the car. When I was able to grab her, I jumped out of the car and ran into the house. I was so sure that this was the end of our relationship. I had my mind made up that this was it and I was not going to tolerate his madness anymore. But as usual, I ran into the house showing no signs of harm and acted as if everything was good. I wore that mask well. Later that night he called to apologize and once again I took him back.

As I mentioned briefly earlier there is a cycle that occurs within the relationships of domestic violence. It's an insane process all within its self. In the middle of the cycle is the word Denial. It is the spoke of the wheel that moves the cycle along. The victim is in denial that the abuse will stop one day and the batterer will eventually learn to love them or at least stop hurting them and the batterer is in denial that this is alright and his apologies should be enough. Many times the batterer also believes that when they say this is the last time that they mean it. It's a revolving cycle that honestly never stops unless someone decides to make a change. Even then there could be just as much danger than if a person stayed.

I am blessed because even though I was a victim of domestic violence I have now had the opportunity to provide therapy to those same victims just like me. As a therapist, I was often asked many times by victims do I believe that their spouse could change if they had anger management or therapy of some sort? One of the biggest questions that victims ask because they want to be with their spouse for the simple fact that they love them unconditionally. They just wish that the abuse would stop completely, so they have hopes of change. And that shouldn't surprise anyone because as human beings many of us believe in the power of change otherwise we wouldn't strive so hard in life to do better. So we know that change is possible but how far do we go and to what extinct do we continue to put ourselves in danger. That's the question? So my answer to them is that we can all change. But we as the victims are not responsible for staying around while they try to change. It is not our place to change them or to continue to accept their abuse while they seek help. We must love ourselves enough to remove ourselves from the situation and heal. If the batterer has the strength and the humility to want something different for themselves, then they have to make that move by themselves for it to be genuine.

The cycle is called the cycle because it constantly revolves around and around and around and around. It never stops, unless someone wakes up and no longer is in denial.

The Engagement

Relationships are fickle. They are about one of the most unstable things I have ever experienced. One day you're in love the next day you hate each other and that's in relationships that are supposed to be normal. So imagine what it's like being in a relationship that is dysfunctional and abusive. Throughout the course of our relationship, we broke up several times and got back together. Every time we broke up I never told anyone what was going on because I always knew within my heart that it wasn't over. I had a few opportunities to break away from him but fear brought me back. Within me was the fear of being alone, fear of being a single mom and fear of limited finances. I began to develop this belief that I would never be free of him. I hated this man, but yet I was in love with him. I thought that I needed him to survive. Insane!

As our relationship continued to spiral downward he came up with this bright idea that we should get married. I did not understand where this was coming from because our relationship was not any stronger, but worse than ever. When he asked me I was hesitant to respond. There were all kinds of thoughts going through my mind which should have allowed my mouth to say no. But the fear of loneliness set in with my brain stating no, but my mouth stating yes. On the outside I showed excitement to cover up my confusion, wishing that someone would have spoken up for me and said no for me, but that did not happen either. One of those moments where I wished that someone would have stood in the gap for me and said, girl, are you crazy. I mean I believe that I covered up the abuse for the most part but someone should have seen how crazy he was or maybe not. Maybe he played his part just right and I was the only one to see who he really turned out to be.

So I went along with this plan of getting married. I thought that when you got married that it was supposed to be a joyous occasion. I thought that it was supposed to be a magical time in people's lives. A celebration of two people bonding as one in love, honesty, and truth. I found myself preparing to get married to this abusive man who hid his anger from the world. I lived this life of abuse in total secrecy. I dealt with every verbal and physical assault by myself. So even though my family might have thought that he was weird I guess it did not give them a reason to reject his proposal to me. When I told my family about the marriage, for the most part, they were supportive. Some had their doubts but they were still there for me. After a period, I convinced myself that this was an exciting time and planning it was going to be fun. So what did I do, I went through the motions of being the happily engaged woman. I did all of those things that soon to be brides would do. I purchased wedding books to get myself in the spirit of happiness. My mom assisted me in planning the wedding. We were moving forward as if everything was great. We scheduled the date with the church, the meeting with the Pastor was arranged and the reception hall was on hold. I knew in my heart that I did not love this man enough to marry him, nor did I want to give him a license to think that he could beat me any more than what he already had done. So why was I going through with this?

As time was passing I began to get more and more anxiety about actually marrying this man. He had been nothing but hateful towards me since the beginning of our relationship. I was not naive to think that once we got married that everything would change for the better. I knew that things would change for the worse if we got married.

In my mind, I had to figure out a plan to get out of being engaged to Todd. So because we argued every day about something my chances of an argument occurring was huge, which was going to be my way of ending the engagement. I just didn't have the heart to do it when everything was fine. Yes! Just call me a punk. But that's ok because this punk had to do something different for herself to take a small step in getting free from these invisible shackles that he had on me.

So I am sure that many of you know about a woman's intuition which is real and we can feel when things are not quite right. More times than not we know when something is wrong and when we should take action. The problem is that we don't always listen to that voice in our head. So with that, I knew that Todd was cheating on me, but I just couldn't prove it at the time. So I began to accuse him of sleeping with other women and when I did that he had the nerve to say that he was a grown--- man and he could do whatever he wanted to do. So even though I was taken back by his statement, while he was yelling and calling me names, I took that opportunity to call off the wedding completely. Amazingly that silenced him for a moment. He responded to me in disbelief, but I continued to make it clear to him that the relationship was over. I was surprised at myself for actually saying those words which had never happened before. He began to get ready to leave and while he was walking out he received a phone call from someone. It did not take me long to realize who he was speaking too. He proceeded to tell her that he was on his way to her house and he made sure that I heard him. Todd already had this date planned before I even broke off the wedding so my intuition was correct. He then proceeded to walk out of the house, laughing. I guess he thought that he made a fool of me but at that moment I did not care. I just wanted that relationship to be over.

I felt liberated that I did something to finally stand up for myself. I thought that this feeling would have given me enough strength to leave Todd completely, but it was not. We split up for about two weeks and I ended up back in his world of lies, deceit, and abuse all over again. That invigorating feeling of hope only lasted two seconds.

What is the answer to healing abuse? Is it marriage? I don't think so. Marriage is not the healer to abuse but a continuing downward spiral of pain. So often we have this belief that if we totally commit in the way of marriage or have a child that this will bring two people closer together. Many people believe that it will solve the problem when in fact, it brings on more difficulties. All this does is add more anger, confusion, and more problems to an already hostile situation. And in many cases, some men believe that you are now their property when you become married, therefore all the more reason to treat you like an object.

Our self-worth has to be more important than anything. In our society, many people define success as being married with kids. They never realize the consequences that could come with this if they are marrying the wrong individual. For many women, the marriage ends up in death do us part, literally. Women are losing their lives to their husband's anger and are dying at rapid rates.

We have to remove society's perception of what is successful and into God's eyes of what is successful. We also know that God calls for marriage but He calls for people that are yoked together and are of the same mind filled with His love. And as I stated earlier, love does not hurt nor does it cause pain to anyone. He said that the husband must love his wife as Jesus loved the church, so we must recognize that these two must go hand and hand. The husband must put Jesus first which will create nothing but love in the home. Love is what marriage should consist of, nothing else. So if you are looking for marriage to be the answer in an abusive relationship, think again.

The Move

Here we go: Abused by Todd since the third day of knowing him. I was verbally scared, physically battered, emotionally traumatized, cheated on and deceived, but yet I still forgave him through it all. And even though I called off the wedding I still decided to move in with him after we got back together. I am sure many people will ask, why would I accept this next offer of moving in with him? That's a question I still cannot answer. But I do know that he had that invisible chain connected to my brain and he was the only one that had the key. I was fighting for my freedom key but I kept failing at permanently owning it. He wouldn't stop calling. He kept using our daughter as a reason to see me. He kept coming over and begging for forgiveness. I was just worn out and forgave him. I was very nervous about being under the same roof with him all alone. But as I thought more about it, this was an opportunity to get out of my mother's home and a fresh start to living as an adult, so I jumped at the opportunity.

So the day came where I took a dangerous leap to move in with him. It was a nice two bedroom apartment, in the same neighborhood which made me feel comfortable. I tried to think positive about the move and not have too much anxiety. I was hoping that he would change now that we were together under the same roof, thinking that maybe some of his stressors were removed. When we first moved into the apartment we both worked full time and he established that he would make sure that all of the bills would be paid on time. The plan was that I would give him a large portion of my check to make sure that everything was taken care of in the household in combination with his check. Because this was my first time living on my own I felt like he was taking some stress off of me. What I did know for sure was that I was a very naïve 21-year-old battered woman looking for something.

While living together, I entrusted too much of my life in his hands. There was an assumption on my part that things were being taken care of and that he was looking out for my best interest. He made everything seem so simple and worry-free. Every month he would place the bills on the dining room table and commence to pay them. I would sit there and watch what I thought were checks going out. I never had a reason to believe that he was not paying the bills each month. Oh, how naïve was I? Why was I surprised to find out that this was not the case? He was very clever in many of his action but yet slow in believing that I would never find out.

The first bill that I found out about not being paid took me by surprise. It was the main source of how we were living. The rent was backed up for a few months. I couldn't understand because we both worked and brought home enough income to cover all of the expenses. And I only found this out because there was a letter sent about late fees and it also listed information regarding possible eviction proceedings. I was furious because I was giving him money every month and things were not paid as planned. When I questioned him regarding this issue, he stated that everything was fine and we were not going to be evicted. He tried his hardest to reassure me that the bills would be paid. I did not believe a word he said and began to go on a search to see what else was behind in payment. A few days later the electric and phone bill arrived and when I opened them up I began to get even more furious because the both of these bills were extremely overdue. All I could think about was what in the world was he doing with my money? So I decided to confront him again since none of this made any sense to me.

Now, believe it or not, I can be a little feisty when I am upset so as soon as he walked through the door I had question after question after question about where my money was going.

When I asked him where all the money was going, he became very defensive and told me that I was not to question him. I was so angry at this point because he would not give me a straight answer and I felt lost and helpless. And even after this confrontation he still expected for me to give him most of my check every two weeks but I had a huge problem with that and slowly but surely my eyes began to open. I tried to change the way in which I turned over my check to him. Because of this Todd became more aggressive towards me, which in turn made me rethink my plan of action. The finances continued to spiral downwards and they never got better. We were in debt with the possibility of being evicted. And because my name was on a couple of the bills they followed me even after we moved on.

Lesson 102: Financial Abuse is real. People are abused in so many ways and never realize the depth of just how bad it can get. Many times we just look at the physical piece as major but all types of abuse can take a toll on a victim.

Allowing someone to totally control my finances was a mistake but I thought that at the time it was the right thing to do. This whole experience created a hole in me for many years of my life. A hole so deep that I would not allow myself to trust anyone with my finances ever again. I was so fearful to be taken advantage of like that. It was so extreme that even something as simple as mailing off a bill had to be mailed off by me. If I was not there to see it mailed off it made me nervous. It placed fear in me so tight that I refuse to share my income status with anyone. I gained an attitude that no one would ever run my life or dictate my money. NEVER!

I like to think that I am getting better with this today because I find myself sharing my finances within my current relationship which is a sign of healing. It all comes down to trust which is high on my approval list. I am learning to break free of that because everyone is not out to abuse. There is love in the land. There is healing in the land and I have been open to it.

Our past can dictate our future if we are not careful. We must be open to new experiences in realizing that people are not out to see us fail. The only way to be free of our past experiences is to allow our minds to be renewed in its thinking and allow God to remove the existing pain that clutter's the heart. We have a right to be set free. It's our God-given right.

Yes! Your Mate Can Rape You!

Society continues to be conflicted on this issues of rape. I see it every day in the work that I do, advocating for survivors of domestic violence and sexual abuse. Women in this world have been objectified and therefore seen as objects so the mindset says that a man has a right to have sex with his spouse anytime. And at one time it was a law that a husband could not rape his wife but we know now that this is not the case. A woman can be raped by her spouse as well as a man can be raped by his spouse believe it or not. Sexual assault is another part of being abused by one's spouse and Todd took advantage of this as well because to him I was his property to treat as he pleased.

One evening Todd asked me to go out with him and a few of his friends. At the time our daughter was out of town with his mother visiting with family in North Jersey. I honestly did not want to go but I went anyway to keep the peace. He was adamant about what he wanted and never really took no for an answer. So we ended up going to a bar that had Jamaican music playing that evening. When we got inside of the club it was dirty and it had an unpleasing smell to it but they were excited to be there. He and his friends began to drink and get high. At this point in my life, drinking and smoking were minimal since I gave birth to our daughter. He kept trying to get me to have a drink and to smoke with them but I wouldn't. As the night passed on I was bored out of my mind, sitting there watching the clock while he danced.

We were there until about 2 o'clock in the morning and I continued to get frustrated and angry. He kept forcing me to dance with him but it was hard to do because he was reeking of alcohol and marijuana. He kept trying to grind on me while we were on the club floor which was embarrassing. I just wanted to go home. I finally opened up my mouth and said let's go. I was ready which made him very angry with me. It still took a little time but we eventually left. Because he was drunk I ended up driving us home. The drive was long because he kept trying to touch me and put his hands up my skirt which was annoying. I kept pushing his hand away but he just wouldn't stop. He loved saying that my vagina was his, therefore calling my body an object. I just kept driving as fast as I could without getting pulled over. I was hoping that he would just fall asleep but that didn't happen.

After a while, as we were traveling home he became quiet until we got to the apartment complex. When I pulled into the driveway he told me to drive around the back of the building. I didn't ask too many questions at that point. I just did what was asked of me to do. As we reached the back of the building he told me to park the car in an area that was dark. I followed his instructions not knowing what to expect. As we sat there I was able to recognize how beautiful the sky was that evening. It had a pretty blue tint with stars sparkling and the wind was calm so it could have made for a romantic evening. While we were sitting in the parking lot he pulled the keys out of the car and proceeded to go to the back and opened up the trunk. I thought nothing of it and therefore I just sat there waiting for him to come back. After a few minutes, he called me out of the car. He had a pleasant tone in his voice so I had no reason to think that something horrible was about to take place.

As I walked towards the back of the car he immediately pulled me by my hair, turned me around and bent me over the back of the trunk. What I did not realize was that he had a thick metal flashlight in his other hand. He then sat it on top of the trunk, kicked my legs open while still having my hair twisted in his hand. Then he began to pull down my underwear and commenced to shoving the flashlight up my vagina. I began to cry and begged him to stop, but he would not. I continued to cry and as I got louder he kept telling me to shut up. Then he began laughing and calling me obscenities. It truly felt like I was there for hours with no ending in site. He kept shoving this metal flashlight into my vagina and pulling my hair to stay still. I can remember pleading with him to stop. Telling him that I would do whatever he needed for me to do but please just stop. When it was over I remember bleeding and being in so much pain but he didn't care. He thought that this was funny. When he was finished raping me we got back into the car and he made me drive to our apartment. It was pretty silent for most of the night until something snapped in my brain and caused a feeling of rage within me towards him. After some time he decided to go to sleep while I sat in the living room angry and in pain. While he was sleeping I couldn't remove those thoughts from my mind replaying the incident of him raping me with this flashlight. It just kept replaying over and over again and the more it replayed the more homicidal I would get. As the rage rose, I had had enough and decided to grab a machete from the kitchen drawer, walked into the bedroom and stood over him holding the knife in my right hand. At that point, I didn't care if he heard me or not. I was out to kill him. I stood over him for some time crying and wishing that I had the strength to stab him in his head but my daughter kept flashing through my mind. Those images of her beautiful face are what brought me back to reality. Once I came to myself, I slowly walked away from him and placed the knife back in the kitchen drawer. After pacing around the apartment for some time, I decided to go to bed. I still don't understand why I decided to lie next to him when I could have slept on the couch. But after sleeping for a while, I was awakened in the middle of the night, being forced to have sex. I could have killed this man that day.

Being raped by Todd was humiliating. It was worse than any beaten I could have experienced. He violated me in so many ways that evening. Violation of my self-worth and every shred of dignity that I had left in me was destroyed. I was embarrassed because even though we were in the back of the building we were still standing underneath somebody's apartment and who knows if they saw or heard us. I felt like I was going crazy in my mind with no way out. I needed to be free from him but I didn't have the strength to leave.

There are so many women locked up in prisons for defending themselves. So many women lost because someone thought it was ok to brutalize them. So many women tortured and maimed because someone thought that they were their property. So many women wounded and scared because someone thought that she wasn't good enough. We as a society have to get better at protecting our women from criminals preying on them and not locking them up for taking their protection into their hands. Now, no I don't agree with murder but we do have to get better at protecting the victims. Restraining orders are just a piece of paper that many times only antagonizes the batterer and makes things worse for the victim so she doesn't apply for one. And because she doesn't apply for one we cannot hold it against her for understanding her situation much better than we do being on the outside. We have to be more proactive in helping those that are suffering and are in bondage. We have to change our minds about how we see abuse and the woman and men that stay. We have to be advocates, leaders, and supporters and fight for those that are struggling with fighting for themselves. We have to interject before it gets to that place of taking either one's life because all life is special. Many of them are just broken.

Battered! Bruised! Raped! Tired! Angry! I slowly but surely began thinking for myself. I knew that this was not the way in which I should be living. Throughout our time together I worked in retail, with no education and no clue of what my future was going to hold. So one day I decided to try my luck in another field and thankfully I was hired at a cable satellite company in Voorhees, NJ. I was so grateful to have something different. My pay was higher and I met new friends that began to give me life. There were all types' of people within this company and I allowed myself to get to know them. It was nice to have friends again.

Even though I was in a relationship with Todd I began to receive attention from other men that I worked with and for me, it felt good to have someone see me. I just wanted to be seen and it felt good that other men paid attention towards me. I would flirt and even thought about entertaining some of their advances. At this time I didn't have any girlfriends because Todd purposefully pulled me away from them. But at the job, I was able to meet a few good friends and we began to spend time and hang out every once in a while. We would have to do things secretly because he was always finding reasons why I couldn't hang out and have fun. He would use our daughter as an excuse for why I was not allowed to hang up with others besides him. But this excuse was only good for me but not valid for him. There was always a double standard within this relationship.

I truly enjoyed going to work because it gave me a sense of freedom. I can remember one day my girlfriend by the name of Jackie and I went to take a smoke break. It felt so good just to laugh and hang out. There was no drama, just pure fun which is what I craved. So as we sat on the curb she began to tell me some things about herself. Things that I was unaware of, not that it mattered. There was one moment where she asked for my full attention because she wanted to tell me something that was very important to her. As she was speaking I could tell that she was very nervous by the balls of sweat pouring from her head. Jackie took a risk by putting her business out there not knowing how or if I would accept her. So as I gave her my full attention she began telling me that she was a lesbian. She also stated that she was afraid to tell me this because she enjoyed our friendship and was afraid that I was going to walk away. So at first, I was surprised because we both would talk about these two guys at the job that we were attracted too. And we discussed how we were going to figure out a way to double date. So even though I was surprised, it wasn't going to change our friendship.

I figured that was the end of the conversation. The big secret, but boy was I wrong. Her next confession took me for a huge loop. She told me that she was attracted to me. Oh, my! Too much information all at once. But I took it all in and listened to what she had to say. You could tell by her facial expression that she was really afraid that I was going to say something hurtful. I would have never been disrespectful towards her for sharing her feelings but I did begin to laugh hard. I was extremely nervous and anxious all of sudden. But after I got done laughing hysterically I said to her that we are good.

I did explain to Jackie that I had never been hit on by a woman and therefore this made me uneasy but not afraid. And after I said that, you could see this sigh of relief on her face. She was very grateful that I wasn't rude to her and still wanted to be her friend. After our long smoke break, we returned to work. Jackie was a good person and I enjoyed her friendship so walking away from her as a friend because of her feelings seemed ridiculous to me.

A few days later I was upset because of the way in which I continued to be abused by Todd. I was always seeking a way out and at that moment I just needed a break from him, so I called Jackie. I was surprised that he was open to the idea of me hanging out with a friend. He was not very happy but open to the ideal so there was not fight around the issue. When it came time for me to leave, Jackie suggested coming to pick me up instead of using Todd's car. I was appreciative and took her up on her offer. Everything seemed normal when she came to pick me up. I said bye to my daughter and to Todd and we left. When we got to her place it was nice. We sat around and laughed. I talked about guys and she talked about girls. I could tell by our conversation that she felt safe and had more freedom to talk about her real self. We began drinking and continued to have a good time in our conversation. Because we were having such a good time with one another she asked me if I would like to stay over and without hesitation, I said yes. So I called Todd to tell him that I was staying at Jackie's house for the evening. Well, he was not happy at all. He began to yell, calling me vulgar names and told me that I better come home tonight. For one of the first times, I did not listen and continue to enjoy her company. We were just hanging out watching movies and drinking. After a while, we went out to the balcony to smoke and out of the corner of my eye, I saw her looking at me.

So I turned to her and asked her, what's up? She stated that she wanted to kiss me, and without hesitation I said, ok and she kissed me. I admit I was intrigued at that moment. It was different. Nothing that I had ever experienced before. The problem was that she wanted more. She wanted to sleep with me. She wanted me to be her girlfriend and I told her that I was not gay. She became very upset because she wanted to believe that I would leave Todd for her. She believed that her kindness towards me was enough but I knew that even though Todd was horrible towards me, we had a family together and at that moment that's what mattered. As some time past that evening, she asked me to stay the night and I did. I slept on the sofa and she slept in the bed. The night started out full of laughter and fun and ended up somber and quite.

That morning I received a phone call around 6 am from Todd. He was screaming at the top of his lungs demanding that I come home now. He was calling me all kinds of vulgar names to degrade me and to degrade Jackie. He accused me of sleeping with her. He was so full of hatred and his language was so disgusting. Todd then began to threaten me. He threatened to take our daughter away from me if I did not get home within the next 30 minutes. I did not have the car so I had to rely on Jackie to get me there. His threats did work because my daughter was everything to me and he knew it, so he used our child as leverage to get what he wanted. On the other hand, Jackie was extremely angry with me for listening to him. She wanted me to stay for breakfast but I told her that I had to think about my daughter and please take me back home now.

The whole way back she did not speak to me and that was the last time that I saw her. Apparently, she was from D.C and decided quickly to move back there so I never saw or spoke to her again. I was saddened by the way things ended because I did enjoy our friendship but I did not want a relationship.

First I was not going to risk losing my daughter to anyone, so if she didn't want a platonic friendship there was nothing more I could do for her. And to make it even worse I got my behind beat when I got home by Todd, so I lost either way.

Bam!!

This relationship just kept going on and on and on. Why? Everything that could have happen did happen and yet I was still there believing in something. What did I believe in? I don't know. Things just continued to spiral downwards and got worse. Every time I thought that I reached the bottom and all I could do was go up, he would surprise me with another blow. Everything just intensified from the arguments, which became longer and stronger, the physical altercations which became even more frequent and the emotional abuse which extended through the roof.

So remember at the beginning where I was telling you about Dr. Jekyll and Mr. Hyde aka Todd. Well here is the thing, every day was not a terrible day. So when I question why I didn't leave, this is part of what kept me with him. He was funny, and at times very playful. So that honeymoon period that I talked about earlier continued to exist and it was a nice space to finally catch a break. I remember this one day where I truly thought that we were going to make it without an argument or a one-sided boxing match. On this day we didn't argue and we laid around watching television for the majority of the time. After a while, we were trying to decide what to eat for dinner and since he enjoyed cooking, it was obvious that the best choice would be for him to cook. He made one of my favorite dishes: curry chicken. It smelled so amazing and I couldn't wait to eat. With that being said, I was betwixt and between due to being excited about my favorite dish and still walking on eggshells. I never knew when the bottom was going to drop. He would change his mood at the drop of a dime.

So the day continued and wouldn't you know, the bottom finally dropped. When he would physically abuse me it would normally be preceded by an argument. Walking on eggshells kept me alert, but I was caught off guard for what happened next. Todd said dinner was done while I was sitting in the living room. He was not yelling and everything was calm and quiet. Nothing happened previously, so I felt good about the day. When I proceeded to go into the kitchen to fix my plate, out of nowhere he punched me in the eye. What in the world was going on? I looked at him in amazement. I didn't understand why he would hit me. I remembered falling back into the wall while holding my face. He just stood there and watched me with no remorse and said nothing. It was as if it was a normal thing to do. Just as normal as taking a shower every day or brushing your teeth. Afterwards, he walked out of the kitchen into the back of the apartment and I proceeded to fix my plate like nothing happened. Now I was standing there in the kitchen, crying profusely, snot running down my nose, with a pulsating eye and I am fixing a plate of food that he cooked. For all that I knew, he could have poisoned the food but I still continued as normal. Insanity at its best! I then exited the kitchen, sat on the edge of the chair in the living room with my plate of food in my hand. I was trying to understand what had just occurred. It is so hard to make sense of abuse but I kept trying. I keep trying to understand the why factor hoping that maybe I wouldn't feel so crazy inside. While I was sitting on the arm of the chair getting ready to eat my food I heard him storm down the hallway towards me. Once he got close to me he grabbed my plate out of my hand and stated that I was not good enough to eat the food that he cooked. He opened up the patio doors and threw the glass plate over the 3rd story balcony. He had no regard for anyone that might have been in the path of furry. He then came back inside and just that quick he pulled out a knife and pressed it hard against my neck. He said to me that he could kill me and no one would ever know that he did it. Here was Satan staring me straight in my eyes. That was the moment where I truly began to fear for my life. I thought that this man had finally lost his mind and that he was ready to take me out of here for good. I felt my heart beating so fast going 100mph. I started sweating as if I just completed a 50 mile run in the dead of summer. Tears were rolling down my face like a faucet. And I told myself in that instant that I was going to be dead if I didn't leave this man. After a few seconds, he removed the knife from my throat and began to laugh cynically. He made it clear that I better not call the police and pulled the phone out of the wall before heading to the bedroom. I sat there for a while in misery. I could still feel the pressing of the knife against my throat. Why? Why? Why? Why have I stayed so long? In misery! In hell! In sadness!

For the very first time, I truly realized that it was time to go. It was time to plan my escape for good. Todd had reached a point that he could not come back from and I had to get out before I was his first body count. There was nothing else that could be done in this relationship. I truly believed in my heart that he wanted me dead. Part of leaving such an abusive situation is planning your escape and it takes some time especially when children involved. So even though I did not leave immediately it took me about another two months before I could get up the nerve to get out but my heart was no longer in it and it was time to run.

Due to being in this field of work for over 10 years as well as being a victim of domestic violence, when a batterer tells you that they are going to kill you, believe them and don't take it lightly. Believe that they are crazy enough to harm you in such a way that is deadly. And if they are crazy enough too physically, verbally, financially, emotionally and psychologically abuse you, then they are capable of killing you. We must understand that we don't know anyone that much to know there every step or every thought against us. We must love ourselves enough to take care of ourselves. If you can, get out before it gets to this point. And if you can't at this moment seek support from one trusted person to help you set a plan of escape so that you can get out safely for the sake of you and your children. God bless you!

Out of all of the things that occurred in our relationship it took this one thing to take me over the edge. In the past, I never called the police because I just wasn't ready to walk away. I wasn't ready to become a single mom but that no longer stood in the way of my freedom. Boldness finally kicked in for me and I just had enough of his manipulation.

As usual, we were arguing and he decided to get very creative. While I was standing near the closet in the living room he charged from the other end of the kitchen with a bucket in his hand. And before I could even say anything or move he proceeded to throw this bucket full of water on me. I was drenched from head to toe. I was so angry. I had had enough up to this point. I had taken so much of his mess over the past 5-1/2 years and I was tired. Tired of being abused and used sexually. I had enough of being his punching bag. So, I picked up the phone and called the police for the first time. As I was on the phone waiting to hear a voice on the other side of the line he came closer towards me and pulled the phone out of my hand. He began to laugh at me as if this was funny. He then said after everything he had ever done to me, how could I be so stupid to call the police because he threw a bucket of water? He continued to laugh and call me vulgar names over and over again. He stated that the police were going to laugh at me, but much to his surprise when the tables turned. Now, I never got the opportunity to speak with anyone on the phone because he snatched it out of my hand. But the good thing was that when you dial 911 they come out no matter what if they don't get a response over the phone.

So after I made the call, I left the apartment, walked outside and sat in the car to cool down mentally and to dry off. As I sat there for a while I noticed when the police came and I watched them as they headed upstairs. I waited to see what would happen. I have heard horror stories about not always being supported in these type of situation so I didn't know what to expect. But when I went up to the apartment to my surprise the police were very supportive and on my side. As I watched his face I saw nothing but fear in him for the first time. It made me feel good inside to watch him sweat. The police were negative towards him and made it very clear that if I wanted to go and file a complaint that I could and they gave me their information. Even though I never pressed charges it was still a win for me because for the first time I got to see him back down and walk in fear. After the police left I received dirty looks all throughout the evening but he was silent.

Who would have ever thought that this tough guy that abused me for close to 5 ½ years was a punk? After this incident, he never put his hands on me again out of fear of going to jail. Wow! Was that all I really needed to do? Threatened him with the police and the possibility of jail time and he would stop. That seemed too easy, too simple. But what did happen was an increase of the verbal and emotional abuse for the last month and a half that I stayed. The impact of verbal and emotional abuse is hard to prove in a court of law, and restraining orders are typically not provided on this basis alone, if there is not adequate proof that it is occurring.

Our system is made up of centuries of beliefs that women are the property of men. Even in the year 2017, we continue to fight for equal rights. Not too long ago men had the right to beat their significant other with a ruler that was not wider than their thumb, i.e. - the saying: "The Rule of Thumb". I believe that the same mentality still exists.

Women have a hard time proving that they are abused. Physical abuse shows the legal system that something damaging is occurring which provides them with proof, but what about the verbal and emotional abuse which is just as harmful and detrimental? Women become discouraged because they are constantly pushed away and re-victimized when they seek out help. Something has to change. We can't wait for someone to be killed before we open up our eyes.

In my case the police were supportive, but that is not the norm. And for our system to grow and develop, we must make it the norm and become better advocates for protecting people that suffer from abuse.

I have a question to ask: is cheating a form of abuse? Yes or No? If you answered yes, then you're correct. It is abuse! Many times we as a society do not see cheating as abusive. We might see it as wrong and unfaithful but not abusive. The mind is very fragile and can become disturbed if not properly taken cared for. Cheating is a form of emotional and psychological abuse. It causes a person to feel less than and worthless. It communicates to another human being that you do not matter. It plays psychologically with the brain that challenges everything that we know to be true and real.

Close to the end of my relationship with Todd, I guess you can say that we had an open one because he was openly cheating on me. He decided to date and have sex with other women with no regards for me. There were phone calls made in front of me, along with physical gestures of what he wanted to do with these women while speaking with them over the phone. After 5 ½ years and a child, I was nothing to him. My presence in the room did not matter. I was kicked out of our bedroom many nights so that he could have phone sex with other women. I would hear him moaning and groaning on the telephone. And mind you that there were times where our daughter was there in the other room while this was all taking place. He was psychologically damaging our daughter and myself for the future. He felt as if I had no right to say anything due to him being a "grown man".

One night he went out and was brutally honest about where he was going. Even though I had enough, this was still hurtful to see and to hear. Who wants to live with someone that is so disrespectful towards them? He treated me like the scum of the earth. The mother of his children. Because I didn't know what else to do this one night I waited at the front of the building, standing by the 3rd-floor window, to see them pull up.

I was torturing myself waiting there to be hurt but I couldn't stay still in the apartment.

All I could think about was cursing her out and doing damage to her because she was ruining my relationship. I was not thinking with common sense that this relationship was over years ago and that she had nothing to do with this. After hours of pacing back and forth to the window, he finally pulled up after midnight. Filled with anxiety and sadness, I couldn't understand why I kept allowing him to hurt me in this way. I kept going through these emotional mood swings. One minute I was ready to leave and the next minute I was depressed wanting him home. Why did I continue to put myself in this space? When he returned home I ran back to the apartment and waited for him to come in the door. As he entered I began yelling and screaming at him. He ignored me and went to the bathroom to take a shower. At that moment I was ready to fight and I began to take things into my own hands, and needless to say, I fought dirty. From this point, everything was out in the open. I began to live as I wanted to live and proceeded to date and sleep with other men. I knew that cheating was not the way to go about it but it worked for me at the time and it helped me to move forward. I made things alright within myself and had an attitude that did not care about anyone nor anything.

I brought men into our apartment when he was at work during the evening. I took chances and had men in our apartment during the day when I knew he was out. I would meet men and sleep with them just because I had no connection what so ever to them. And towards the very end, I got bold enough to tell Todd that I was cheating and did not care about the consequences. What I did not expect was for Todd to try and gain something from these different situations. What I mean by this is that he wanted me to sleep with other men for money so that he could benefit as well. His proposal totally took me by surprise. Basically, he wanted me to be his whore. I went along with it for a brief moment only to back down later. There was an incident where he was pressuring me to set up one of the guys so that we could get money out of him but I refused to go through with it. I was afraid of Todd, but I was not willing to be sold. So I dealt with the consequences by continuously being verbally abused. My plan back-fired but it didn't stop me from cheating. I just learned how to become a better liar.

My life consisted of hatred and rage for others. I was so angry at the world and felt like a failure. Inside of me, I felt as though I had been living a life of pain and suffering and I was filled with rage and needed someone to take it out on. My brain was disturbed and refused to be controlled. I failed to realize that he was still controlling my actions because the only reason I was responding that way was to spite him. What I needed to learn at that point was that anybody that can change your mood and cause harm to you, has control over you. I had to learn how to shift the controllers in order to move on.

One day someone asked me a question: They asked me what was the cheating all about for me? Where did the desire to sleep with other men come from? After a lot of thought and going through the healing process of my past, it opened up my eyes to why I lived this way for many years of my life. Sexual abuse and Physical abuse can truly do damage to the mind of a victim. It gave me a screwed perspective of who I was because I did not feel worthy enough to care about myself. All my life I have been looking for love. Looking for someone to connect with me. Looking for someone to want to be with me. Looking for someone to cherish me and make me feel important, but I was a broken mess. My heart was deformed. It was beating but it had no life. I lived recklessly. I would meet men at the bus stop and get into their cars only to continue to be treated as an object and used for sex. Not thinking in my right mind that I could have been killed searching for love and crying out for help. Sleeping with a taxi driver that I just met because I needed someone to pay attention to me. I needed someone to make me feel special. My new drug of choice was SEX!

As readers from all over the world read this book I am hoping to reach as many women and men that have been yearning for love and never receiving it. So many men that I slept with and none of them filled the void that I had inside of me. None of them gave me the peace that I desired. None of them made me truly feel special. None of them made me feel like I was the only one that mattered. None of them held me tight and close to their heart. None of them were interested in my dreams. None of them gave me purpose. None of them gave me a reason to live. None of them took the time to truly look at me. The only thing they did was provide with a false sense of hope. Hope that they were the ones.

We have to stop giving ourselves away to others that will only throw us back into the wilderness. We are not objects to be thrown away. We are precious in Jesus sight and we deserve more. We deserve to love ourselves and to give ourselves the love that we have been so desperately seeking. We have a right to be heard. We have a right to be seen. We have a right to be loved. And we have a right to make our demands and to provide all of these things for ourselves. We have that right!

The End

It was finally coming to an end and I was at a point in my life where I did not care anymore. Being a single mom was no longer a fear. I was praying to be out of this relationship forever. After the incident with the knife to my throat, I was mentally preparing to leave and that time had finally come.

The day was here. The day of restoration and freedom. The day that I thought I would get my life back. The day that I was free from him. It was here! It was around 12:30 at night, our daughter was away with his mother for the weekend and the apartment was quiet. I took a shower and put on a pair of cut off shorts and a t-shirt. Even though I was preparing to leave mentally I had no idea that that night was the night. Todd and I had some conversation but nothing that would indicate that my departure was coming. I began to do my hair because I had plans of meeting a male friend. Like I stated we both now had an open relationship and I no longer cared. It was all on the table and up for grabs. What did I have to lose? Nothing!

It's amazing how when the victim decides to cheat how the cheater responses in anger. Why did it even matter to him that I was going out with someone else? Once again, abuse is all about control and Todd had finally lost his control. As I was preparing to leave he stood in the doorway of the bathroom and asked me where I was going. With no fear in my voice, I proceeded to tell him that I was going out with a friend. He then questioned who this friend was and when I explained that it was a male friend he started yelling. Todd was making demands that I better not leave our apartment or else. The term or else no longer mattered. I continued to get myself ready and as I was headed to the front door he stood in front of me and stated again that if I leave I better not return.

Wow! At that very moment, I was able to breathe for the first time in over five years. It was as if I was waiting for him to say those words all along. It finally clicked! I struggled walking away from him but I guess I just needed him to walk away from me which is how I took it and it worked finally. The only words I said to him was ok and I proceeded to call my mom and asked her to remove the chain lock off of the door. She wanted to come and get me but I told her no. I would make my way there but I did not explain what was going on at the time. I was never actually going out with a friend but I just needed a way out and I got it. I saw the open window and jumped out quickly landing on my feet. He opened the door and for the last time, I walked through it, never to return. I truly believe he thought that I was not strong enough to leave him, this is why he did not put up a fight. There was no way he took me seriously. He truly thought that I was bluffing but the bluff was on him because I was gone.

As I was walking outside leaving the apartment, I could remember thinking to myself, is this really over? Was I so lucky to walk away from this insane relationship with my life? Many women never get to experience such a smoothed transition of being able to walk away. For a moment I remember looking back to see if he was following me because this just felt too easy. This man did not enjoy losing control, so there was no way he was going to let me walk away without a fight. At least that's what I thought to myself. But thankfully I made my way to my mom's house safely by bus with only a pair of shorts, a t-shirt and my purse in my hand. I had reached my bottom and it was time to go. But I was smart enough to know that he was not done trying to get me back, so I prepared myself for his antics.

The next morning he called from work apologizing and asking me when I was coming home. For the first time, I stood up for myself and stated that the relationship was over. I explained to him that I was going to get clothes from the apartment and that my decision was final. I felt so liberated and strong. I never allowed myself to go back to him. I slowly started to understand my self-worth. I never felt so relaxed in my life when I finally decided to move out and go to my mother's home with my daughter. There was peace within me that I could not imagine would have filled my soul. He tried with all of his might to tear me down to its lowest levels and for the most part he won, but I could not allow him to take all of me. I always had a fight within me but I never knew how to properly execute it. Being in this relationship did teach me a lot about myself. It was my first serious relationship outside of college which provided me with insight on life and life's trials and tribulations.

This was the longest 5 ½ years of my life. He did everything in his power to degrade me, to ridicule me and tried to destroy me but he didn't win. I got out alive and so can you. We as survivors have to realize that we are just that: Survivors! We have survived the worse of the worse and yet we can and will thrive towards higher heights. I was blessed to come out with a sane mind and be able to get my education and help other women and men that have endured some of the many similar trials that I have experienced. Life was not easy doing it alone and having to figure everything out myself as a single mother. Actually, at times, I thought about going back because it got hard, but I realized the strength within myself and kept moving forward.

One of the hardest things to face was my own anger that was developed throughout the many years of trauma that I had experienced. That was scary to admit, but I had to face it in order to get better and become whole. I was so angry with Todd for so many years and it showed in my own behavior towards others. So after leaving Todd, my journey had just truly begun.

As a professional, I seek to help others with understanding the need for taking care of themselves before getting into another relationship. Sometimes when we find an escape from someone and not allowing ourselves to heal properly, it can cause a whole lot of issues in the future. In doing this work what we are finding is that many women are now becoming the batterers due to the anger and rage from the past or present relationship. It's that volcano exploding all over again which is hurting everyone in the process.

Wounded

Abuse can be so debilitating. Being unable to think and move effectively. And because of all of the rage that was pent up inside of me since eight years old, I found myself on the other side of the fence. I became the aggressor. I became what Todd was to me; that ultimate form of hatred and I, in turn, hated myself for it. I trusted in no one, I believed in no one, and I hated everyone especially men. And one would think that with such hatred fuming within me that it would have distracted me from getting back into another relationship so fast, but it didn't. I should have never tried to open my heart to another man so soon but I did and it was a mess.

I found myself in a new relationship with a man that I was infatuated with as a child. His name was Ronnie and I always thought that he was so beautiful. But can you imagine how excited I was when we reconnected again as adult? I can remember it like it was yesterday. It was about 12 midnight and my cousin and I was hanging out in Camden. While I was sitting on the step of a friend's house I saw him out of the corner of my eye walking up towards me. Honestly, it was like a dream come true. A childhood crush manifesting itself after all these years. He looked at me, I looked at him and we hugged so tightly. We began to take a walk as we held hands and from that day forward we were enmeshed. Here lies the problem: he had just got out of prison for selling drugs and I had just got out of prison. The prison of abuse! So we were both wounded and a mess and you can only imagine what happens when two messes get together. They only create a bigger mess.

So there I was with Ronnie in all of my madness. I hated that he used drugs so I took all of my rage out on him. I was determined to make him feel the pain that I felt for so many years of my life. I went into fits of rages and basically, I reacted like a fool. How could this be? How could I become my past? I recognized the pain that my abusers placed on me. I remembered the physical pain that I felt when Todd would punch me in the eyes. I continued to feel the knife up against my throat. I remembered the fear that was inside of me due to all of the physical, verbal and emotional abuse. So why with all of this in the forefront of my brain, would I put another human being through the same type of pain? The rage inside of me created some holes of its own. My behavior was embarrassing but just like my abuser covered up himself to the world, I also learned how to do the same. I could not allow people to see what I had become. To the world, I was kind, funny, generous, happy and loved life. At home I was hateful, deceiving, dishonest, disloyal and plain ole ignorant.

I had become very emotionally abusive in which I started to cheat and sleep with other men. In the beginning, I tried to be faithful and loving but it wasn't working. I still lived as if I was in that relationship with Todd. I still functioned as if he was in my life. What I realized was that Todd still continued to have control over my mind even though I was no longer with him. How could my mind continue to be ruled by him? Even though I was physically out of the relationship I was mentally still in it. I continued to cheat and live a life of hate and disgust. I also became very selfish. My life was mine no matter what anyone wanted. I felt as if my past relationship suppressed my inner self. I could not give my heart or any part of it to anyone at that time.

Things had to be done my way, in my order, with my consent and nothing or no one could change my mind. The way I reacted was the response of a wounded person. And when you are wounded you do things that are reckless and many times insensitive.

As I look back on Ronnie and my relationship I knew that he always loved children. He would always light up when children were around. He was a child at heart and wanted more children. The problem was that I struggled with the thought of having a lot of children and I did not have the same desires. So he kept asking me to get pregnant and I would say no, but yet I took no precautions to make sure that did not happen. Therefore because we were very sexually active I got pregnant four separate times and I had four abortions. Yes, you heard me correct: Four! I was living raggedy and very irresponsible. Ronnie continued to get very upset because I took no thought of his feelings and terminated the 4 pregnancies. I was very rude and careless. After the first one, he left me for a brief period within our relationship hoping that I would feel some remorse and understand how this affected him. But it happened three other times, which left a hole in his heart. I truly had no concern about how he ever felt about my decisions, but yet he stayed. We functioned in such a dysfunctional manner and I could never understand why he stayed with me during this wounded state of my life. I was 26 year years old but yet I had a mindset of a 10-year-old, throwing tantrums and not taking accountability for none of my actions.

Now, I feel like it's only fair to say that Ronnie was not perfect in anyway. He had issues of drug abuse, emotional and psychological abuse towards me but nevertheless, it did not warrant my behavior towards him at all. We were just two hurt unhealthy individual's trying to make things work but ended up hurting one another. Anger is not a good recipe for a good relationship and we were both angry, selfish and clueless.

Anger! Rage! I call this the volcano effect. It destroys like a volcano. Volcano's sit and fester until they get to the point where they can't suppress it any longer and they erupt with lava and destroy everything in their sight.

Rage destroys when we don't deal with anger in a healthy way. Anger in itself is healthy. It's not the anger that gets us in trouble but how we handle our anger. Many times our anger turns into rage and we explode. Coming from a victim's standpoint, we get to a point where we are tired of being abused and taken advantage of and all of those years of hurt and pain come to a head. We destroy those that are in our way. Many times there's limited concern for the new relationship, the children or people within our circle. We have to learn to seek out help when we are free from the abuse and allow ourselves to gain back our self-confidence and self-esteem before we move forward in another relationship. Otherwise, we will end up sabotaging it. We must take time for ourselves and either capture the love that we never had for ourselves or regain the love that we once knew for ourselves. It's imperative.

Also, my reaction to Todd's actions towards me is why I am so adamant about helping individuals understand the importance of healing within themselves before moving forward into another relationship. We could damage any healthy man or woman that comes along. We must truly find that unconditional love for oneself and then and only then will one be able to have a healthy and trustworthy relationship. We need to fully understand that we have a right to heal and be healthy in every way. Jumping from one relationship to another will never allow for anyone to seek deep down within themselves and mend those issues. Coming out of an abusive relationship one must learn how to be alone and sit with those lonely feelings. At times the pain will seem extremely overbearing as if one will not be able to move forward, but those are only irrational thoughts. Sitting with the loneliness is a must, for it is only temporary. Your loneliness will tell you that you cannot live without him or her, which we know is not true because our lungs function and our heartbeat without the help of another individual. But what is true is that if you continue to stay in an abusive relationship there is the possibility that it will kill you.

Let's not become the new batterer. When we respond in the same manner we are now continuing the cycle of violence. We must learn to give ourselves permission to be set free and be healed.

Looking at self, was one of the hardest things that I ever had to do. I had to recognize everything about me that was wrong and not blame anyone else for my issues. I wanted to believe so bad that it was entirely Todd and the others perpetrators fault, but I couldn't. I just could not blame all of them that have battered me for my actions. I had to be broken. It wasn't until I thought that I lost everything that I finally sought God and when I sought God, He lifted me up in a manner that I could have never imagined. He allowed for me to see how beautiful and wonderful I was and that He loved me with all of His heart. I never experienced a love like that before. It didn't judge me nor did His love condemn me. I had to learn to let things go and most importantly I had to learn to forgive. I had to learn how to forgive others and to forgive myself. What a powerful learning experience for me this was which inevitably set me free. Forgiveness gave me a new life and it can give anyone a new life if we seek for it. I never really thought that I would be able to reach this place of freeness. But after all of these years of pain, frustration, anger, rage, lying, cheating, and deceiving, the ultimate refuge was soul-searching. Seeking God has given me the ability to move forward and not live bound up in my mess and for that I am grateful.

Listed are some red flags to watch out for that could characterize a possible batterer. Please do not look at this as an exhausted list.

1.   Possessiveness
Individuals who are possessive tend to be extremely controlling. They are interested in keeping you all to themselves and controlling your every move. Sometimes a big mistake is that the victim sees the possessiveness as flattering due to the constant phone calls and the individual's need to know their whereabouts on a minute by minute basis. But this possessiveness is only a way to control and provide them with more leverage.

2.   Jealousy
Jealousy is not healthy. It is another form of control. Usually, people who are unable to control their emotions have low self-esteem and therefore their emotions come out in negative ways. Jealousy is neither cute nor flattering. Be careful of an individual who constantly accuses you, questions your whereabouts, and seeks to keep you at bay.

3.   Belittle Your Thoughts
No one should belittle your thoughts for they are your thoughts, which makes them important. Name calling is another form of abuse. Anyone that has to make you feel less of a person is not worthy of your time nor your space.

4.   Secretive

If a person is secretive about their life, this is something to be concerned about. One of the biggest parts of being in a relationship is being able to share and learn from each other. But if that person is secretive about who they are I would suggest that you keep your eyes and ears wide open because something could be wrong.

5.   Cruelty to Animals

Anyone who abuses animals more than likely has an anger problem. Most of the time this anger is not limited to animals but to anyone that gets in their way. A person can only hide their true self for a short period, so eventually, they will show their true colors and take their anger out on their spouse.

6.   Lying

Many perpetrators tend to lie about the smallest issues. They are unable to hold the truth within themselves, therefore when questioned their abuse comes out on the individual.

7.   Blames Others For their Problems

Individuals who abuse tend to blame others for all of the problems that have occurred in their life. They never take responsibility for anything. According to them, their downfall is always the cause of someone else. Be aware.

8.   Objectification of Women

Many times perpetrators look at women as objects, as if they are not a person, but a thing to be thrown around and made less important than a man.

Knowledge Is Power!

What Prevents individuals from Leaving?

There are many reasons that prevent women and even some men from leaving an abusive situation. Society thinks that it should be easy to pick up and leave but it's not that simple. Here are some reasons why:

• Financial Reasons
In many instances the dominate partner usually controls the money, leaving the victim with no means of supporting themselves if they wanted to leave. Many times they see no real alternatives and staying with the abuser seems worth it to have the financial security. Lastly, many victims who have been in abusive relationships for a long time and unemployed do not possess many skills that would allow them to be employed and raise their family on their own.

• Fear
There would be that ultimate fear of intimidation and threats by the abusers if she or he was to leave. As we know statistics show that many victims are more likely to be stalked or sought out if they leave home. Over the past couple of years, there have been more reports of homicides when the victim finally gets the courage to leave. So many times a victim is in more danger if she leaves than if she stays. There is also that threat by the perpetrator of wanting to commit suicide which places fear in the victim.

The victim stays so that the abuser does not hurt themselves. Then there is that fear of losing the kids, which when the perpetrator loses control he seeks to get at the one thing that the victims love and that's their children. So fear of losing the children is huge and therefore keeps victims in the home.

• Isolation

The batterer will often isolate the victim from the outside world which also includes their family. This would leave them with no support if they wanted to run. Batterers will many times threaten to kill the victim and the children if she or he tells anyone or tries to report them to the authorities. The friendships developed by the victim are usually cut off and destroyed by the batterers. Many relationships are broken between friends due to them not being able to handle the abuse, especially being on the outside looking inward.

More than Physical

Domestic violence is more than a physical act, which is all that society often sees. It consists of much more damaging things such as verbal abuse, emotional abuse, mental abuse, financial abuse and sexual abuse. Verbal abuse is very common in relationships but sometimes difficult to identify. Batterers have a way of damaging a person's self-esteem while acting as if they care about them. They are controlling individuals with their words and making victims feel less than a person. Verbal abuse consists of name calling, threats of harm, and blaming, along with the use of profanity, yelling and screaming. Manipulation is also a tactic that can be used in controlling their spouse. It is extremely damaging to a person's self-confidence and self-worth, therefore, could do just as much harm as physical abuse.

Emotional/ Mental Abuse is another common form of abuse that is hard to prove and hard to identify. Jealousy and possessiveness is a huge form of abuse. This is when the perpetrator isolates their partner from their family and the world. Isolation provides them with the upper hand in making sure that their spouse doesn't leave and they don't lose control. Extreme jealousy is a way to keep the individual from socializing with anyone other than the perpetrator. Emotional abuse also means that the perpetrator works to place fear in the victim by being reckless, intimidating and stating threats of harm.

Sexual abuse is another form that is overlooked within marriages/relationships because society still believes that a woman does not have the right to say no. No means no in any realm. She should not be forced to perform any act of sex against her will. She has the right to have sex with protection if she chooses to do so without being forced to get pregnant or possibly getting a sexually transmitted disease.

These forms of abuse are overlooked and are just as serious as physical abuse and should not be belittle. Within our legal system, there continues to be a need for change because victims are being re-victimized two, three and four times over in defending themselves to the world. Why do we continue to ask, "Why do women stay?" instead of asking, "Why do men abuse?" The blame and the responsibility to change continue to always be placed on the victim. Ultimately this needs to change. The responsibility needs to be placed on the batterer to change.

Domestic Violence is a serious epidemic and we as a society must take it seriously. Women, men, and children are dying every day at the hands of a batterer and we have to stop looking at this as if it's a family issue. Domestic Violence is a worldly issue and it must stop now. Please stand with me in Solidarity and become an advocate for survivors of domestic violence and sexual abuse. Let's not make them fight alone.

Here the reality: this is my story but this is many women and men stories and some make it out and some don't.
So please speak up!

Cycle of Violence Wheel

Tension Building Stage
Abuser starts to get angry
Breakdown in communication
Victim feels the need to keep the abuser calm
Tension

Denial

Acute Explosion Stage
Any type of abuse occurs
Physical
Sexual
Emotional
Threatened
Suicide

This cycle continues around around around someone it.

Honey Moon Stage
Abuser apologizes for the abuse, some beg for forgiveness or show sorrows
Abuser may promise it will never happen again.
Blames victim for provoking the abuse or denies abuse occurred.

to go and and until stops

Sometimes the cycle doesn't stop until the victim is murdered. Other times it takes the victim to finally leave and come out of denial.

Scene 3
Free

I wish I could be free from worrying about my weight. Constantly trying to hold up to a standard of beauty, which is impossible to hold. Trying to immolate what the world sees as beautiful. A hole that I will never be able to fit into. For one I am a black woman, so the world tells me that I do not compare to the standard of beauty. Second, my lips are big and my skin is dark which also does not hold up to the world standards of beauty. Third I am fat. 3 strikes against me. How could I ever win? How could I ever compare to the standard of beauty? I am empty. I walk around every day like an empty shell. I appear to be excited and fulfilled but I am empty. People seem to compliment me more when I am thin and now that I am fat again nothing but silence. When I was thin I was reassured that I would find a husband but now that I am fat again what does that mean? Does it mean that I will be lonely all my life? Does fat equate to being unattractive? I don't like what our girls see and what they are being told and fed on a daily basis by the world. Why must we conform to the world's ideology that thin is beautiful? When I look at myself in the mirror, I see an overweight woman! An unattractive woman! I don't like her! I don't like the way she looks! She disgusts me! I don't want to be fat anymore, but it's such a roller coaster, up and down, up and down, up and down. I'm tired! I'm worn out! It's making me sick! I hate the scale! I want it gone! It controls my mood! I need its hold to be released from me. I want to live beyond the scale. I want to live beyond what the world says about me. I want more for myself. It's time to be free from the pain. I am tired of the world telling me what's beautiful and what's not. I am so tired! I just want to be me and live free!

On November 20, 1973, I was turning one year's old. I remember seeing pictures of this little girl with pigtails, wearing a ruffled dress, sitting on the table. We lived in the black and white house in North Camden, New Jersey. My parents threw me a birthday party and during the party apparently I was missing in action, but they knew that I had to be in the house somewhere. When they found me I was under the dining room table and guess what was in my hand? It was a stick of butter. Wow! Of all things to eat, I was eating a whole stick of butter. Being a therapist I was prone to analyze many things, so I saw this as a metaphor for a welcoming presentation of my life to come. I was told this story from my family. And I see this as being prevalent in the course of the rest of my life when it comes to food and the hold that it had over me.

So, who was this beast that I am referring to in the title? It's called Bulimia Nervosa. Bulimia was a beast that I battled for many years of my life. It took control of my every emotion and thought. Being overshadowed by this disease nearly took my life in such a slow but powerful way. Growing up I never knew that this existed or that it even had a name. I recognized that there was a problem but I did not understand the depth of its destruction.

In my culture, having an eating disorder is not recognized in comparison with other cultures. We weren't taught about Anorexia, Bulimia, or Binge Eating. We constantly diet as well as exhibit those behaviors within these disorders but yet we don't recognize them. We don't connect with the damage that overeating does to our bodies. We see it as practicing what we love and modeling what we saw from our parents. I listen to my grandmother talk about how when she was growing they had to eat whatever was made and placed on their plate. And a lot of that contained food that was full of fat and sodium. So what I learned what that this same mentality was passed down from generation to generation. Whatever was prepared for you to eat, you ate it and you didn't complain about it. You weren't allowed to pull yourself away from the table if you were full. That just didn't exist especially if you did not want to get in trouble. So as I see it, there was no such thing as binge eating in our family because eating a lot was considered healthy and acceptable.

In my family circle, we never needed a reason to get together. Most of our get together consisted of eating good food. It was everywhere and what made it so hard was that my family could cook very well. They were chefs in their own right. So imagine fried chicken, barbecued chicken, fried fish, baked fish, stuffed fish, hamburgers, hotdogs, sausages, crabs, macaroni salad, macaroni and cheese, potato salad, sweet potato pies, pound cake, banana pudding, monkey bread and so on and so on and so on. It was like our little piece of heaven when we got together. Makes your mouth salivate just thinking about all of this amazing food.

Now, as I take a look at some of the African-American culture today, many of us still live this way. Even though some of us are starting to become more health conscious due to the ever-growing diseases such as Diabetes, Heart Disease and High Cholesterol, as a whole we still lack in this area. The fact that we are killing ourselves and don't even know it is such a hurtful thought. We have the tendency of making excuses for our health and not accepting the fact that many of us suffer and cover up our feelings with food. Yes, we know that drugs and alcohol are a huge coping mechanisms, but food, I believe would run neck and neck in regards to how we cope negatively. It makes us feel good inside. It's like an explosive feeling that soothes the soul and makes an individual comfortable and relaxed. It's legal and acceptable so therefore we all partake in this addictions. And to make it even worse we support each other around this addiction. We tell each other, you're not fat, you're just big boned. We enable one another in destroying our bodies and somewhere it has to stop because we are killing ourselves softly.

What is Bulimia?

The term Bulimia Nervosa is a disorder characterized by recurrent episodes of binge eating. Having feelings of no control and therefore overeating during the binge. Self-induced vomiting, use of laxatives or diuretics; strict dieting or fasting or vigorous exercise to prevent weight gain; and over-concern with body shape and weight (Ruderman & Besbeas, 1992). According to the Diagnostic and Statistical Manual of Mental Disorders (DSM-IV), it requires two binge-eating episodes a week for at least three months to make a diagnosis. (1)

Understand that there are some people that do not fit this exact explanation. Self-induced vomiting is one of the most prevalent ways in which a person would purge after tossing down 10,000 plus calories in a short period of time during one sitting. Often one will act in secrecy, and they feel disgusted and ashamed as they binge. They are relieved of tension and negative emotions once their stomach is empty again (American Psychological Association, 2011).

Bulimics understand that their behavior is out of control and therefore causing even more stress. Laxatives in high portions are also taken to the extreme to relieve the body of the high caloric diets. Bulimics tend to fear gaining weight, therefore they become compulsive with getting on the scale. The scale runs their life and their mood for the day. If the scale looks "appropriate," then their day is somewhat good until the next binge occurs.

It's hard to recognize a person with Bulimia because usually, their weight is normal, unlike Anorexics. Food becomes their every thought for the rest of their life if not controlled. It is an addiction just like any other addiction. The only problem is that one needs food to survive, so it is constantly all around them. Food is teasing and taunting them as if it will never cease to end. The exact understanding of what causes Bulimia is not known but there are factors that can be looked at such as genetics or family influences, or chemical imbalances. These could be an issue, along with possibly cultural factors where health and thinness is a constant concern. Bulimia is a silent killer that many individuals are suffering from on a daily basis and if it is not confronted it can end in death.

Confusion is the best way that I could describe growing up in two homes. My parents separated when I was four years old; therefore my time was split between the two of them. During the weekends I was with my father and during the weekdays I was with my mother. They both had different philosophies about food and how it affected our bodies. So you can only imagine the confusion that it caused. I had an unhealthy relationship with food and just like everything else it tried to ruin my life. It sought to control my every thought. And its grip on my life was worse than any grip than any man could have ever had on me. Now that's serious all in itself.

Here is what it looked like as a young child going between two parents. During the week I was made to eat everything that was placed on my plate whether I liked it or not. In one household you were not afforded the option to decide what you liked or what you didn't like. There was a mentality where my mom worked extremely hard to make ends meet, therefore we had to eat whatever was prepared, no compromising. There were all kinds of things in our cabinets ranging from healthy food to not so healthy food. I saw fruits of all kinds, along with cakes, cookies, and pies as well. There was also a showcase of different diet items within the cabinets as well, which I partook in secretly. I always felt as if there was a sense of wanting to look better and never being satisfied with myself.

I can remember sitting at the dining room table for hours at a time. Sometimes it would be daylight when I started to eat and as time passed and I would look up and it would be 9 pm and I would still be sitting there. Sometimes my mom would sit there and if that happened she would force feed me. And other times I would be alone and those are those moments where I would begin to get very creative. The trash can, the washer, and dryer began to know me very well in that a lot of my food would end up behind them.

On the weekends when I went to my father's house the situation was different. Body image was also an issue but in a different sense. He had many discussions with me about what was healthy and how unhealthy foods could affect the body. When meals were prepared I didn't have to eat everything and if I tried to force the food down I was told to stop. Most of the cabinets had more healthy items and less sugary items. After some time it began to get very hard because of the mix messages.

So for me, this was an every week process, back and forth with mixed messages about food. One minute I was forced to eat everything and the next minute I was forced to stop eating. How do you decipher all of this information from your parents? What's right and what's wrong? What's healthy and what's unhealthy? Where does your commitment lie in regards to obeying either one of them? I would always mess up week after week because I wanted to please them both but it began to get hard when I was being told different information on a regular basis. Eat this, don't eat that, taste this, and don't taste that. Confusion could make anyone go crazy in their mind. Part of my problem was that I flocked more towards the rules in my mother's home than in my fathers. Sugar became my best friend so it was hard to give it up when I went back to my dad's on the weekend, so I would begin to hide what I ate.

My dad was into being healthy and therefore he worked out every day. I don't think that my dad had an ounce of fat on his body. So I can remember as a child going to the park and working out with him. I was not in shape at all as a child and the furthest I ever ran was probably to the kitchen or up the stairs, but that was it. So when we would go to the park he would have me running with him. To be so young I was always out of breathe. And then I would get pains in my side from all of the running. I would want to stop and many times I tried, but I was encouraged to run through the pain. So with these mixed messages, food became my companion that failed me in the end.

I was aware of the fact that I was a fat kid. I hated it. I never liked who I saw in the mirror. Every time I looked in the mirror all I saw was this fat ugly kid. And even if I didn't think that I was fat, I was reminded of it daily. I was constantly told that I was putting on weight and that I needed to watch what I ate. I can remember going to my grandmother's house that passed away some years ago. She would always have a can on her piano filled with cookies and every time I went there this was the first place that I would go after kissing her. The next step was going grocery shopping. Now we would not leave her home to go shopping, but instead, I went to her basement where she kept all of the goodies for me to explore and take home. I was given a paper bag and allowed to fill it with applesauce, cookies and more cookies, along with cakes that she bought just for me. I grew believing that this was good for me. My life consisted of food, food, and more food. Everything revolved around food. I would then be confused because after I would "go shopping" sometime later I would get the conversation about being chunky and how that was not fitting for a young lady.

So at such a young age, these messages consumed my brain. Please understand that I am not blaming anyone for being bulimic, I'm just stating facts about what occurred and how my unhealthy relationship with food began.

Mixed messages can confuse anyone of any age. It can bring a false understanding to an already confused mind. As children are growing they need to be able to feel secure within themselves. Having feelings of being overweight can set a child up for low self-esteem all through their future. We as adults have to be conscious of how we speak to children. Those ugly, little names like chubby, pudgy, thick, Pillsbury dough boy, big momma, and much more are horrific to a child. That central processing place in the brain doesn't understand how to separate cute pet names from reality, therefore it all stems from the truth and causes deep shame and embarrassment.

Children need to have a sense of safety. A sense of knowing that no matter what they look like on the outside that they are loved. This love can continue to cultivate a child to be filled with high self-confidence and therefore a sense of self-worth. Providing an amazing future to a child that might feel a little different than what society says they should look like.

The Struggle

From as early as 12 years old, I can remember wanting to lose weight. I had a negative self-image of myself. I was never able to see beauty through my own eyes. I was broken in every way and never understood my purpose for being born. There was a sickness that I felt in the pit of my stomach every time I would glance at myself in the mirror. I felt like I was disgusting. Having those feelings of loneliness and disgust for self, food became my partner in crime. I needed to have it to fill that void in me.

Sugar! Sugar! The ultimate killer! It provides us with a craving that is so unbearable and hard to break. Sugar is in everything, even things that we couldn't imagine. When I was in a binge mode I craved sugar, I desired sugar and yearned for sugar. The feelings were euphoric. What many don't understand is that sugar is worse to kick than any other drug including marijuana, cocaine, crack, heroin, etc. Sounds crazy, but there are many facts to prove this statement. And the worse part about it is that we are feeding this to our children every day, with no thoughts of changing.

I believed that I was addicted to sugar. I would experience those urges out of nowhere, but I never could comprehend what was happening to my body. I needed it, wanted it and if I did not have it, I would get very angry. Sometimes within our house, we did not always have what I wanted such as cakes, cookies, and sugary things, so I would handle things in my way. I'm not proud of it, but I can remember stealing money from my mom so that I could get a sugar fix. Sounds like a true drug addict and I was, but my drug of choice was sugar along with alcohol and marijuana.

One day mommy's pocketbook was sitting near the couch and she was upstairs. All I wanted was a few dollars to take care of my cravings. But because I was stealing it, I was moving fast and when I ran out of the house I realized that I took a $50 bill. I was scared to put it back because I didn't want to get caught, so I kept it. After a few minutes, I went to the corner store where I was trying to hide the money. I ended up buying tons of penny cookies and candy. There were some of my friends at the store as well and when they saw me with this $50 bill they wanted candy as well, so we all walked out of the store with a bunch of junk. As I was on my way home I felt like I was high because I ate all of that stuff in a matter of minutes, scarfing it down my throat. For one I didn't want to get caught with all of that junk food and second it was a craving that I wanted to fill quickly. I ended up getting caught anyway because one of my so-called friends told my brother that I was at the store spending a lot of money and he in turn told my mom. From there she looked in her pocketbook and realized that she was missing her money and I received one of the worse beatings of my life. All I wanted to do was to fill a craving that I knew no one would understand if I tried to explain it. We don't realize how addicting sugar is and how it can affect our thoughts and behaviors.

I talked about how I was raped multiple times previously and due to this I struggled with my emotions and understanding how to cope at times. In the middle of the night, alcohol and marijuana weren't always within my reach but the food was so I would hide it in my bedroom for those desperate times. When I could I would purchase snacks at the corner store and hide it while bringing it into the house.

I would have it in my closet, under my bed and even in my drawers so that I would have some form of comfort with me at all times. As I mentioned earlier, the food was my companion and a huge source of relief. Some nights I would sit in my closet crying for hours, eating whatever I could find. There were times where I would end up falling asleep in there as well. I can also remember some nights waking up in sweats from nightmares and reaching under my bed for cake or cookies which helped to relieve the pain of being afraid. So this became normal behavior for me.

Throughout those years my imagination grew and I learned how to create calmness to rid myself of the hysteria that was going on in my life. As a child, I spent many nights afraid of sleeping and being alone. I would change my room around often in hopes of creating a new world, a world filled with peace, a world filled with no pain. The room that I slept in was an average size room, so I was able to maneuver it in different ways. When my bed was placed directly in front of the door I could see the hallway while lying in my bed. Many nights unable to sleep, I would stare out wishing that my life was over. I had no clue of how to release it. So my imagination would give me a sense of relief. And when that did not work the food under my bed, in my closet or the kitchen always seemed to do the trick. Eating was my savior.

When I was 16 years old, I was able to get my first summer job. I was working at the local drugstore right around the corner from my house, so I was able to walk to and from work. When I first starting working there everything was fine. I enjoyed having a job even if it was part-time. So after a few weeks, I found myself having those desires to steal from the store but I constantly fought them. I was having multiple cravings for sugar and the urges increased over time. I began taking one candy bar, then two candy bars, then a bag of candy bars, then eventually I was taking money. And all I brought was things that had sugar in them and I continued to hide them in my bedroom. I never understood why I did these things. But thankfully I never got caught but I was happy when the summer was over because the craving kept getting stronger and stronger.

I spent a lot of time alone trying to understand all of my actions and why food consumed me. Some days I was without money and resources to stop my craving, so I would find myself going through the cabinets and the refrigerator to try and find something to ease the pain. In the back room of our house, we had this huge freezer that I would search in hopes of finding something but never succeeded. There I was, this miserable child, on the floor in the corner of the room, curled up in tears. There was no one to rescue me and no one even realizing that I was there. I did not understand why I was feeling this way and I couldn't resolve the pain.

It was the year 1990. By this time in my life I was raped multiple times, mugged, suicidal, food addict, a marijuana smoker and an alcoholic all by the age of 17. To the outside world, I was apparently fun to be around, categorized as loud, crazy, always laughing and a part of the "in" crowd. I recognized my future as being bleak, but somehow I made it to the 12th grade. During this time in my life, I was depressed and angry and no one ever recognized the hurt child that I had become. Even though I covered my pain, there had to be something seen in me that would make someone question and therefore intervene. I was defiant but in reality, I was a scared little girl searching for help. Expressing my feelings outwardly was not something that I did. I covered up my true self and wore a mask for most of my life. There was no way that others could see what I truly had become because if they did they would not like what they saw.

During this year of my life, my family moved from Camden to the country, which I dreaded. It was my senior year and I begged to live with my Aunt in Sicklerville so that I could continue my education in Camden at Woodrow Wilson High School. The begging paid off. I was allowed to travel back and forth to school. I would get up about 5 o'clock every morning so that I could get dressed and catch the bus to Camden just so that I would not have to live in the country. I know that this was not a good idea in retrospect because it gave me more freedom in school to cut class and do whatever I wanted to do. It was my last year in high school and it was very lonely, but I did everything in my powers to make it less stressful.

I only saw my mom on the weekends. I missed her a lot, but I would never express my feelings to her. I didn't care about life and what it entailed. I was not motivated to do anything. I just didn't care. I truly did not care about myself. What was there to care about when the rest of the world treated me as nothing?

High school was a challenging time in my life. Within this environment, people usually had a place to settle. What I mean is that there were different cliques. They extended from the kids that were considered to be nerds to the smart kids or the group that everyone wanted to be a part of, which is known as the cool kids, and then you had those that were considered outcast or had behavior issues. I didn't know where my place was, so I placed myself wherever was appropriate for that moment. Not truly fitting into anyone's group, there were many lonely days that I spent in fear of myself not understanding my limitations or strengths. Physically there were always many people around me. Not too many that I would have considered a friend, but more so associates. The people close to me never saw my pain. I covered it up by being loud and disruptive. In the class yearbook, I was voted as the class loudmouth. What a way to cover up one's pain and divert the attention off of the reality that was living within me.

How can we take a closer look at our youth without judging their character? Why are we afraid to talk to our young people? Young men and women are crying desperately for someone to notice their pain. Many times they have learned the trade of Masonry. Building up their own brick walls around themselves to stop the hurt from coming in and/or being seen by the outside world. But we have a responsibility to our youth. We must work hard to not see their rough edges as being defiant but as a call for help.

How can we help them? We must understand that they are not our miniature selves. They have their own unique minds and ways of doing things. But they do have emotions that are overpowered by rage, hurt and pain and unless we intercede they will continue to spiral downwards.

We must stay involved in their lives. High school years are so hard and unpredictable. One minute you are a part of the in-crowd and the next minute you are obsolete. They need support that can help them grow and not feel useless.

Lunchtime! For many, it was a fun period, recognized as a time to get away from classes and the monotonous routine of school. People were free to be themselves and many times acted out in one way or another. On the other hand, it was always a nervous time for me. I never understood many of the feelings that were going on inside of my body. Every day was not the same. Some days I was alright eating around other people and then there were days where I would be fearful of eating with people around. On those days I would find myself not eating. Starving myself was a form of punishment, so I would eventually walk away from the crowd and deal with the pain alone.

One of my favorite places was a few blocks away from the school. It was the local bakery. This place was amazing because you could smell its sweetness from blocks away. It was like your little piece of heaven. The sugar that consumed this place was such a relaxing force that took me over every time I walked into the building. It mesmerized me internally. Sometimes I would stand at the counter and just breathe in the smell before I ordered. The smell was a fix all on its own. As I mentioned earlier, I learned at an early age that the craving for sugar caused what I know now to be anxiety and when I got my hands on it the cravings went away. The days that I would experience those feelings I would make my way down to the bakery so that I would be at ease. I would purchase as many pounds of cookies that I could with what I could afford. I would gorge on as many of them like a raging maniac before anyone would even see me or ask for any while on my way back to school. It was like a strong craving, a fix that needed to be satisfied.

I also know now that those cravings imitated those of someone that has a drug addiction. All the signs included the shakes, the nervousness, and the wants and desires to be filled, and the wide need for a fix. If not fed, the emptiness was painful physically. I don't know if my body was hurting or if my mind was playing tricks on me. Either way, it was horrendous to experience.

The days were bad when I didn't have any money and the anxiety hit full force. I would find myself searching through couches and in corners to find a piece of silver or maybe even a dollar bill possibly. While in school I was always looking down in hopes of someone dropping their money so that I could settle those hurtful feelings inside. I hated those days because I felt useless. Man! Why couldn't someone just recognize my pain and help me? Was that too much to ask for in receiving just a little help from someone? But the bottom line was that I was invisible. No one saw me, they just saw what they wanted to see. Nothing! One of the most defining moments within this disease occurred one day and it had nothing to do with craving sugar. Things got out of hand and my pain turned into anger inwardly. It was lunch time and a few of us went out to get something to eat from the panzarotti truck. These things were amazingly wonderful but extremely fattening, filled with grease that would drip through your fingers and down your hands every time you took a bit. Cheese and red sauce would ooze out of the bread pocket, along with being filled with pepperoni.

Well, after we all purchased our food we went back into the building and commenced to sit and eat our lunch. About 15 minutes later I began to get filled with that feeling of anxiety. Inside I felt myself shaking and unable to sit comfortably. I felt like I wanted to cry and hide under a rock but was afraid to show my true emotions around others. I didn't understand where it was coming from or how to get rid of it other than what I have learned to do previously in this instance. As I stood there with my friends, I began to go into a state of panic. During this spell of feeling erratic, I decided to leave them, not knowing where to turn or what to do. I found myself back outside at the lunch truck in which I now purchased three more panzarottis. And I began to feel embarrassed and alone.

Why would anyone do this to themselves? I knew that I could not go back into the building where my friends were and eat this in front of them. So to be alone, I went to the back of the building where I found a corner that seemed away from the rest of world. There were three of these things in my hands. I sat there on the ground and ate all three of them in a matter of minutes. I felt so sick and scared about what had just occurred. I began to ask myself, why was I doing this? How could I just have eaten four panzarotti's in less than a half an hour? What was wrong with me? Was I crazy? Was I greedy? What was wrong? And what I also noticed was that the feeling that I felt still did not go away. Now, I have just added more pounds to this overweight shell and felt so disgusted with myself. Then within a matter of minutes, it came to me. There was a way to remove all of what I had just ate and it can relieve that feeling of anxiety.

Where I was sitting was a trash can, so I decided to place my fingers down my throat and began to heave heavily. At first, nothing would come up, so I kept trying, which made me place my finger deeper and deeper down my throat until finally, the food began to be released. After it was all over, I felt a sense of relief and that feeling was gone. It was amazing! It was as if I found a new way to get what I wanted but also a way to remove it from my body. After doing all of that I knew that I could not go back to the school because some of the vomit spilled onto my clothes. I cut school for the rest of the day and hung around until it was time to go home.

When I got home I remember feeling sick and just wanting to stay to myself. I could not comprehend what took place that day and only wanted to be set free within my body but didn't know how to do so by any other means. I have no idea how I graduated from high school. This was a mystery to me. I was in turmoil by those negatives thoughts that kept me down. It passed by like a blur. I was unable to decipher what truly took place over the course of that year. Was it real or was it an illusion? Did I make it through on my own merits or did they just push me through to get me out of the way? I wonder!

The College Years

Going through life continued to have its many ups and downs. College played its part in molding my mind and determining my negative actions. It was another place that fed my feelings of wanting love and understanding of myself. In this conquest of searching for self, I continued to live impulsively and compulsively. There was not much thought for what I did and how I did it. There was a reckless side of me that lived on the edge and pushed everything to the limits.

Impulsive! Being impulsive led me down a road of drinking in large amounts. Amounts that were excessive and seen in individuals that were addicted. Would I have called myself someone with an addiction to alcohol? I would have to say yes. I was also smoking marijuana every day as well. It also took the place of purging in many ways, even though I would still binge on food every chance I got. Bingeing on its own never took away the anxiety, so something always had to follow and in this case, drinking and smoking became my tools for coping. Just about every moment of the day consisted of alcohol and marijuana. My compulsive actions of drinking and smoking excessively led me further and further into a state of depression. The anxiety level within me was so high I would find myself fighting from within.

Because of my actions, a decent college education continued to spiral downwards. The more I drank, the less I attended class. The interesting part about not attending class was that I became delusional in believing that I would still past. I missed about 75% of classes and I guess I expected a miracle to save me even though I did not put in the effort. Therefore, the less I attended class, the lower my grades began to drop. And with all of this happening around me, not once did it come to my mind about what I was going to do if I got kicked out of school.

All I wanted to do was search for ways to get high and be free in my body because the pain was too hard to bear. Ultimately that was my only goal. And seeing that everyone that I hung out with was just like me, there was no accountability to anyone. But what I didn't realize was that everyone was not like me and they were going to class and passing. I was missing finals and just doing whatever. The only thing that matter was finding relief from the pain.

In living recklessly I found myself also being promiscuous. There was a sense of relief and a false sense of security for me as well. The attention that I sought and found from men was not real but while in those moments it provided a space that was not a fantasy but reality for a second. Giving myself to them made me feel like a woman inside. It captured the wholeness that I continued to cry out for, but never truly received. So I kept sleeping with one man and another man in hopes of finding it. I can't explain what it was but I can tell you that I never found it. I was not a naïve girl but I did put up a front as if I was this strong empowered woman. I would sleep with them, get what I needed, and walk away as if it never happened. I built this wall with my two hands. Ten years of labor and nothing to show for it. There was neither checking's nor savings, just a bunch of negative deposit slips.

I can remember at the beginning of my college year, I was only seventeen, taking a walk through the mall by myself. At that time I didn't know anyone other than my dorm mates, so I decided to roam across the street alone. As I went in and out of the stores unable to purchase anything, I met this man. He had to be in his 40's. He was the store manager in one of the clothing store that I entered. He began having small talk and it made me feel wanted. A few minutes later he asked me for my number and we equally exchanged information.

Afterward, he asked me would I like to come over for dinner to his place and I said, yes. Now up to this point, I have known this man maybe 10 minutes and already I have agreed to go to his house for "dinner". Later that evening, he came to pick me up from campus and we went to his house. I wasn't at his house maybe 15 minutes when he began kissing me and we made our way up the stairs. In no time we were naked and having sex. There was no dinner involved, just sex. Afterward, I can remember feeling dirty but on the outside, I had a different response. I was more aggressive and wanted to know where the money was since I slept with him. He looked at me like I had two heads. I then put on his robe and went to smoke a cigarette but was redirected to go downstairs to the patio because there was no smoking in his home. Not soon after that, he took me back to the dorms and I never saw him again. The sad part about this was that I don't even remember his name even if I wanted to tell you. I lived my life this way for years. In and out of different men's beds, cars, alleyways, parks, wherever. Searching for love and coming up with nothing. When I got back to the room I binge on food and alcohol. I was so angry with myself for continuing to disrespect myself. Continuing to allow others to disrespect me.

I spent many nights drowning my sorrows in alcohol, marijuana, food, and sex. I was addicted to all 4 and they ruined my life. I would crave them simultaneously and would find ways to fulfill all of them every time. Sex I could find anywhere on campus or off campus, so that was easy to fill. The food was all around me whether in the cafeteria or our dorm room, also easy to fill. For some reason, I had a large tolerance level for alcohol, being able to drink straight liquor and guzzling the bottle.

And because I could do that, people were always amazed at my ability, so for many nights, I would receive free alcohol. Things like Gin, Grain Alcohol (100%) proof, E&J, Vodka, it didn't matter, just as long as it wasn't a mixed drink. And my best friend and I had a guy friend that lived in New York who would bring us weed every week. Enough to last us, so I never had to pay for that. So my needs were always fulfilled in those areas and it just increased. No one stopped me, they only cheered me on. I had never received so much attention especially from being able to drink so much and not falling over. I was always able to hold my own and the more I drank, the more they cheered. I had a false confidence that only took me deeper into depression.

During the last semester of college I managed to binge on food every single day, drink compulsively, get high on a regular basis, get pregnant, had an abortion and lastly to top it all off, I got expelled from college due to receiving all F's. I was a mess! Oh yes, I was a hot mess. Having my first abortion when I was 20 years old was a mess. The father of the baby was a good friend of mine from school who became my boyfriend on the low. What that means is that no one knew about our relationship. I don't know why it was a secret but it was and I do believe that he loved me and that I loved him. But I could not have a man's baby especially since I was dating this guy in jail back home. I knew that he was getting out soon and having another man baby was out of the question. I was also not ready to have a child. I was a child myself. This guy was not happy about me getting rid of his child but he had no say in the matter. At the time I felt like it was my body and I was going to do what I wanted to do. So it was hard for him to accept and it did something to our relationship. And since I wanted the abortion I only asked him for half of the money and I had a friend of mine give me the other half.

The experience of having an abortion was not pleasant. It was horrible. When my best friend and I pulled up to the building there were protestors outside trying to discourage us from going in. For a moment I thought about it but it only lasted for a minute. When we went inside, there were other young ladies there waiting to have the same thing done. It was like a revolving door, going in and coming out. I was scared out of my mind and I started to think about what if I did not make it out? What if I started bleeding excessively? Would they do all that they had to do to save me or would they let me die? Even though I had all of those negative thoughts, I did not turn around. What helped me to stay was the fact that we got high before we went to the center. As they called my name and took me to the back I began to sweat profusely. The time came for them to do the procedure in which they gave me something to put me to sleep and it was over before I knew it. Just that quick the baby was gone and I felt horrible. So when we got back to the dorms my boyfriend at the time called and wanted to see me but all I wanted to do was to get high and drunk. So I had to choose and I chose to feed my addiction and saw him later. He became secondary.

As I mentioned earlier, I was also expelled from school which should have been no surprise to me. It led me to believe that I was living in a fantasy world that told me I was invincible. And when you believe that you are invincible, you tend to live recklessly. At the moment of realizing that I no longer could attend this college, it filled me with anger for everyone that had harmed me throughout my young life. In my mind, there was no responsibility on my part for my current actions. I began to blame my whole life on every single man that had ever touched me inappropriately and was out for revenge on myself. I was 20 years old and had no future. What was I going to do and where was I going to go?

The Beginning of the End

As I returned home and began to think about my life, it was hard, sad and depressing once I realized what I did to myself. What was I going to do next? The trauma that I experienced just enhanced my anger. It enlarged the void that I was trying to fill with eating. After the abusive relationship, I became so angry at the world that I began to express it outwardly towards others, as well as taking it out on myself. Bingeing on food became a part of my daily life. It was my companion. In high school and college I learned to deal with my anxiety through alcohol, but when I got pregnant, I decided to stop drinking and smoking altogether. My crutch was hard to give up. I went through a brief withdrawal period after I stopped, but I was able to stand the pain on my own without having to go into a rehabilitation center for alcohol abuse. Looking at life head-on as a single mother, with no education other than a high school diploma, felt like I was doomed to fail. I hurt myself in every way possible.

During the heightened period of fighting this disease, I was married, with two children and trying to make something of myself. No one had a clue that I was struggling with this disease. And as usual, I was able to hide my addiction and function in life as a normal human being. Well, as normal as one could see it anyhow. It was so hard to function properly but I managed to play it off. Sometimes it was easy to do because my marriage was in trouble from the beginning. As I mentioned before, he was addicted to drugs and I was addicted to food and neither one of us knew just how bad the other was suffering. We argued over everything, especially money. We were in a rut and therefore both of our addiction got worse. Up to this point, I was just bingeing but my anxiety continued to increase, so somehow I learned about laxatives.

Laxatives became the next way in which I purged. It was different because unlike vomiting and getting that instant relief, this took a little longer but was very euphoric. I can't for the life of me remember how I came to know that these could help me because they were perfect. I could binge on thousands of calories and release. I started out by taking three at a time which in the beginning worked. Because of the wait time with laxatives performing in my body, the relief of the anxiety took longer. Over time the use of the laxatives had to increase to continue to be effective. So I went from taking 3 to 6 to 10 a day because the more you use on a daily basis, the more your system needs to work within one's intestinal tract. As the laxatives increased the cramps inside my stomach increased. But I continued because the benefits outweighed the pain that I endured. I could binge on calories as high as 10,000 and not gain a pound due to the laxatives.

Within this addiction, I was attached to the scale. I weighed myself every day. I could not disconnect from it. Every morning I weighed in, and then when I got home from work I weighed in, and then after dinner, I weighed in and lastly before I went to bed I weighed in. And this cycle continued every single day, which tortured me. It ran my life. If the scale looked good then I had a somewhat good day, but if it was one pound over then life was over. It dictated many aspects of my life. Things that I still can't explain. It was my predictor on how everything was going to be and I needed for it to either be the same or less. And if the scale increased, then the amount of laxatives that I took increased.

Over time the compulsiveness just increased to the level of hiding food. I would purchase certain things just for me and for them not to be eaten, I had to hide them. The problem was that I could only consume them in secret because if anyone saw what I was eating (including whole boxes of cereal along with boxes of something else in a matter of 20 minutes or less) this would have caused an alarm to go off in their heads. Sometimes if I couldn't get away, I would eat a whole box of cereal and chalk it up to my menstruation coming on. And then I would take a box of cakes into the bathroom to eat the whole thing without being seen. It was hard hiding my life from the world. It gave me a feeling of loneliness. As an adult, I was sneaking out to get a fix, a food fix. The only difference was that my fix was at the convenient store.

As discussed previously, sugar was a big deal for me. As weird as it sounds, bubble gum was a huge source of sugar that I craved. It was an instant sugar rush that nothing else could provide other than eating it straight out of the sugar bag. I would purchase anywhere from 50 to 100 pieces at a time and I would consume them all in a matter of minutes. In some ways, this was embarrassing and such a waste of money. I would spend $20.00 or more every time I went to the store, just on bubble gum. And I would do this several times a day. I could spend anywhere from $40 to $60 a day just on gum. Can you imagine spending this in a day on gum? And I would swallow them one by one consuming my intestine with an unhealthy substance. This was about 300 pieces in my system a day, which would explain my many cavities and stomach aches that I had on a daily basis? The cravings at times would begin to get so strong that I couldn't wait for the laxatives to kick in. I never understood until the end of this battle that I was seeking an instant rush of sugar which is what the gum provided.

I spent many hours away from home, which began to give a perception of cheating in the eyes of my husband at the time. Due to my fears, I did not have the heart to tell him what I was going through, so I continued to keep it to myself. Many days I found myself at the store purchasing large amounts of food, sitting in the parking lot alone crying and bingeing. For example, a daily binge would consist of a large pizza, large fries and a sandwich in which I would sit in my car and gorge it down and afterward I would consume high amounts of laxatives. When I ate this much I would take 20 laxatives at one time to make sure that I would not gain a pound and it worked. This was my daily ritual as my anxiety increased. The large amounts of laxatives would cause me to be in so much pain. I never slept a full night for about eight months. Every night I was up with unbearable cramps and was stuck in the bathroom most of the night. Physically I would get the shakes and break out into a deep sweat. My body would also break out into hives due to the excessive amount of laxatives in my system. Unable to sleep, many times I would pace back and forth downstairs wishing that the pain would end. The pain would bring tears to my eyes but not enough for me to stop doing this to myself. This cycle of madness just continued regularly. The stomach pain never totally went away but it did get a little bearable during the day.

Each day brought about new challenges in that I never knew how intense it was going to get. I started to see problems in my ability to do my job. There were issues around me being attentive and faithful to my family and giving them the necessary focus that they needed. I was always tired and craved sleep but never got what I needed due to my addiction. It got so bad that in searching for something to eat I would find myself looking through the trash can just to relieve the pain. The first time that I did it, I did not realize what I was doing until one day when it clicked. I was picking through the trash in a rage. I wanted sugar and I couldn't find it. So I was looking everywhere to find what I needed and that included seeking through the trash until I found something to eat. Who was I? Did I even recognize this person? This person has gone insane. How did I get to the point that I have lowered myself to eating out of a trashcan? And even though the trash came from inside of my house, it still disgusts me when I think about it. What a way to live! Searching for food out of the trash to calm a binge. Now that's an addiction!

So I thought when was this insanity going to end for me? Years and years of bingeing, vomiting and taking laxatives. Tearing down my body slowly. I was killing myself. Pain that just would not diminish held me down and kept me captive. I was in what felt like hell. I couldn't see an end. I honestly thought that I was going to die this way. And with all of the stress and pain that I felt, I don't know if I secretly wanted that to happen. Dying seemed so much brighter than having constant pain figuratively and literally. The negative thoughts just would not go away. But I would smile and take care of my family like clockwork. It was one of the most miserable times in my life.

So the time had come, my final binge before I decided to seek out help. I was home at the time, alone and desperate. I couldn't begin to explain what triggered the anxious feelings. But what I remember doing was pacing back and forth from the kitchen to the living room, from the living room back to the kitchen, over and over again. I had been in this space before which always led to the same results, but I didn't know how to change it. Next, I found myself planted in the kitchen cooking four hotdogs and baked beans, loaded with butter and sugar. While waiting for it to get done, I ate three large bowls of cereal. Right after that I made and ate two ham and cheese sandwiches, and then after that, I consumed the hotdogs and beans. And lastly, I consumed whatever junk food that was on the counter. I was so sick afterward and my stomach felt like it wanted to explode. But the anxiety did not go away, therefore I began to have a panic attack and it felt like I was dying. My breathing was excessively hard and I just couldn't stop crying. It was overwhelming at that moment. I truly felt like a mad woman that had finally gone insane. At that instance, while yelling and screaming, I began to pray to God, seeking His help. After I calmed down while sitting on the floor in the kitchen, I immediately was led to my insurance card for help under the mental health division. When I got up the nerve, I decided to call the number and the process for receiving help was explained. They were very helpful on the other end which made it a little less threatening. They began to explain how many sessions were involved and therefore referred me to a therapist in my area. With fear trembling inside of me I decided to make the second call. I had scheduled with a therapist right away. I did not hesitate when it came to reaching out for these services because I became truly afraid of myself and the impulsiveness that was in me. I was tired of being tired all the time. I was tired of people asking me what was wrong with me. I was tired of my husband questioning my actions and secrecy. I was tired of feeling like an outcast to the world. I was tired of feeling as if I was about to lose my mind. I just became tired of everything. I believe that I had finally hit my bottom. So with being so tired, it was time to make a move and I did just that with no hesitation. I was ready to confront all of my past.

Some of us within the African-American culture have a hard time excepting help from a mental health professional. There was a false belief around how they could help someone. Our perception of them was distorted based on history and knowledge from others around us. This distortion continues to keep many people away from seeking emotional support for themselves. We continue to do a disservice to our healing process.

Being a mental health professional has helped me to understand the need to help and the desire to fight for others. I've been asked many times how I got into this profession and why? Some individuals cannot understand the purpose and the need to help others. I fight to educate people on a daily basis to heal themselves so that they can let go of their past. This battle I will never cease to let go. Our purpose in life is to give what we have within ourselves to one another.

Let us begin to fight for better health whether psychically or mentally because it's all important to our well-being.

Hope

The time had come for my first appointment with the therapist. I must admit that I had a negative perception of therapist and whether or not they could assist me. I didn't truly believe that they could help but I went anyway because I was desperate for help. So as I walked into the office I had a barrier up. I was a nervous wreck being in that space. It felt as though everyone was staring and making judgments about me being there. I'm sure that this was only my fears running ramped. As I was called to the back to meet with the therapist it seemed as if this was the longest walk ever. Dead woman walking, is how I felt. Walking towards my timely death. I didn't know what to expect from them or how they were going to accept me. When I walked into the room I was expecting this long couch on one side and the therapist sitting across from me in a chair wearing glasses with a notepad in their hand. It was eye-opening to me when I found out that none of this was true. The therapist was open from the very beginning and there was no Freud couch in her office. She did not try to psychoanalysis me nor did she make any presumptions about me from the beginning. She began to ask questions about my background and where I was from. I was not very open about myself because I did not trust her. I did provide some information about why I was there and some of my concerns. Most of the time in her office was spent with me staring out the window in silence. The therapist continued to ask questions but I was not forthcoming with information.

By the end of the session, she talked about removing the negative coping skills that I used in regards to purging and the importance of doing so. Lastly, she made it clear that if she was going to help me that I needed to be a little more open in expressing my feelings. When I left her office there was some frustration within me, but overall I was able to manage those feelings and continue to strive for healing.

Our second session was not much different other than me telling her about my bingeing and purging episodes. As we discussed this more and more by the end of our session she came to the conclusion that she could not help me. Her response to me was that I had a full-blown addiction which was beyond her scope of services. At that moment I felt hopeless as if no one could assist me. She then discussed the possibilities of me going to a treatment center and the benefits that it could have on my life. The therapist believed that I needed help that was more focused on dealing with Bulimia. She was ethically unable to refer me directly to a center but slid me a card of where one of her other patients attended. I didn't know what to think at this time. It took everything in me to come and see her and now she was telling me that she could not help. What do you do with that information? Do you just give up? Do you move forward? When I left the office there was a huge part of me that felt a sense of relief due to believing that there was a place that could finally help me. I never knew that this type of facility existed, so even though I was nervous, I was elated. This feeling that I felt was hopeful that maybe someone would finally help me.

But then there was that other side that said, black people don't do this. We don't go to treatment centers for food. That's insane. Eating is what we do, not get treated for it. My brain was going back and forth with these negative thoughts, then with the positive thoughts. It would not shut up. Was I going crazy? It sure felt like it, but I had to take control because what I realized was that I was worth it. I was worth getting help.

The Funeral

As I was driving home from the therapist office, I began to find myself going into a pity party. I was so angry at the world for mistreating me this way. Why was there another issue occurring in my life? I felt like I had enough rough times but here was another one. They raped me, they raped me, and they raped me. They did this to me, so why am I continuing to suffer. He punched me, he slapped me, he tried to slit my throat, and he raped me. Why was I being punished for their deeds? Why was I being made the mascot of trauma? I could not understand the purpose of being consumed with so much turmoil and affliction. How one person could have so much happen in their life? All the way home I could not stop crying. I cried and I cried and I cried, but after all of the tears had been gone away I came to myself and decided to come to an acceptance.

During this process, I felt as if a funeral was about to take place. Healing was about to take place. I was not going to have the ability to binge and purge in the manner that I have been doing for many years of my life. What was I going to do? How was I going to function in society as a fixed individual? How was I going to function as a whole individual? I didn't want to bury the love of my life. We had been together since I was one year old, eating butter under the dining room table. How could I give her up? Food has been there for me ever since I was a child. She protected me from the bad people in my life; she extended compassion and understanding towards me in those lonely times. She never judged nor doubted my abilities and has been that amazing lover that loved me for me. So just the thought of having to bury her killed me inside. I began to mourn and cry even more than ever. She was about to be buried and I had to grieve on my own. I had to let her go.

So before I truly committed myself to attend this treatment center (based upon approval of insurance), I was going to have to have a funeral for her. But before that happened I went on what I called my final fix or so I thought. I binged on every possible thing that was in my sight. I went to my favorite stores, along with purchasing about $25.00 worth of bubble gum to consume. I continued to stuff my face as if there was going to be know tomorrow. I allowed the common sense part of my brain to die and I went into a panic state. Of course, I did not realize that going into the treatment center was just the start and that my addiction was not going to stop automatically just because I checked myself into the facility. I was distraught and filled with anguish over the possibility of losing her. So to help with the added anxiety I cried out for her, hoping that she would stay. However, I understood the importance of allowing her to die, and how it was critical to my well-being.

I knew that there were concerns about my health and that my aunts and mom were seeking answers from other family members that were closer to me. My husband was also struggling with figuring out what was going on as well. I truly thought that I was hiding my addictions. I thought that no one had a clue but obviously, something was wrong, otherwise, they would not have been prying for answers. But I truly understood their concerns because the use of the excessive laxatives caused some physical outward issues in my appearance. All of the laxatives began to drain many of the important vitamins and minerals out of my body, therefore caused my skin to become darkened especially under my eyes. I was also extremely tired as well, and not always coherent. But no one ever asked me directly if there was a problem. I wonder why they never asked me. Should I have been important enough for them to take a chance on me and ask? I didn't think that I was a hard person to speak too but no one asked?

So as I finally returned home from the therapist, my family was sitting in the living room and I knew that I had to tell them. At that point in my life my husband, children and I were living with my mother while we were waiting to move into our home in Camden. I had already come up with how I was going to tell them about my addiction. There were all types of emotions flowing through my head from fear to relief. Fear that they would not understand my issues and why it had gotten this far and relief that I could finally stop moving around in secret. I was tired of living this way and ready for a change. I began thinking that maybe I could finally get some sleep once I get through this program. I was hopeful of it working.

I truly felt like this was my last chance and it had to work. So when I told my husband what I was going through he was upset that I did not trust him enough to tell him what I was dealing with. It took him a moment to get himself together, but eventually, he was supportive. I also knew that since I had made the decision to go into a treatment program that I was going to have to talk about my issues out in the open to the rest of my family. As I pulled my mother and a few of her sisters to the kitchen table the atmosphere was intense. They had no clue what I was about to reveal to them so there was apprehension on some of their parts as well. As I began to explain my current state of affairs, I began to get more and more nervous due to what I perceived as them showing negative facial expressions. For the most part, I felt like it was accepted and understood, but I could tell that there were some questions that needed answered. I was not looking for anyone to totally get it because how could they understand an issue that I could not completely comprehend, but I was grateful for the support. Their support gave me the strength and energy that I needed to go forth in entering the treatment center.

The only problem was that because this issue was now out in the open, I was being watched Every time I ate they watched me. When I went to the bathroom they watched me, when I got up late at night they watched me. I did not need to be watched but understood. I was not a thief but sick. I was not suicidal but sick. I was not destructive but sick. I don't believe that they saw this in the beginning stages and it hurt more than helped.

The Treatment Center

There I was beginning the process of this new and scary endeavor that I could never imagine myself taking before this time. To see if I qualified for this center, there was an entrance interview. I also had to get approval from the insurance company, which took almost three weeks. While being interviewed by the psychiatrist, I felt as if I was mentally insane. He had the typical Freud office with the long couch, glasses and a notepad in his hand. His conversation with me was very brief but very clear in the fact that I fit the criteria of being in this program. He explained the details of the center and what my responsibility would be if I entered.

There were many aspects of the program. I had to attend one on one therapy, see the psychiatrist every couple of weeks, and be a part of the art therapy, group therapy, family therapy, and music therapy, along with seeing a dietician and being watched while I ate on a constant basis. In this place, the rules were very simple. I had to attend all of the groups, and it was prohibited to go to the bathroom before one hour after you have completed dinner. And lastly, every day that you attended program it was a must that everyone got on the scale. How much we weighed was monitored every day. The center included individuals dealing with Bingeing, Anorexia and Bulimia. With all this in mind, I had to now prepare myself for the next step.

When I left that night, all of this seemed pretty intense and overwhelming. At this point in my life, I had a huge problem with people controlling my every move. They were individuals giving instructions on what you could and could not do while you were under their supervision. I was so angry with myself because my sickness got so bad that I had to resort to being in a rehabilitation center. I hated having to rely on someone to help me. I felt like all of my power was stripped away.

A few weeks after being approved, I decided to make preparations for entering the center. It was an outpatient center that called for me to be there Monday thru Thursday, 1 pm until 9 pm. I was not sure how I was going to work this into my job schedule. I was truly blessed in that the individual that needed to approve my absence was very close to my heart, and therefore, in turn, gave me the opportunity to get the help that I needed. The department understood and allowed for me to take the necessary time needed for the next three months.

We as a society are fearful of committing to those hard decisions in order to take care of ourselves. It's a struggle to admit that we have a problem but it's worth it in the long run. We cannot look at our behaviors as being who we are but we must look at them for what they are which is just that, a behavior. Behaviors can change if we put the work into it, but it's a decision that only the individual can make. We must believe in ourselves that we are greater than what has been put out there about us. We are worth giving the best to ourselves and accepting nothing less. This is what it means to admit to a problem and then doing something about it. It's hard but it's right. It gives the individual the opportunity to finally stand up for themselves and say, "no" to worthlessness, "no" to self-destruction, "no" to the mental abuse and hatred towards oneself and "Yes" to the beginning of our new life.

The Walk

The first day at the center was overwhelming. When I pulled up into the driveway I began to get nervous. I thought that I was about to have a panic attack. My breathing began to get heavy and I began to sweat profusely. After I was able to calm myself down I started to walk towards the building and as I got closer I saw a lot of young Caucasian women outside. They looked like they were teenagers. I felt out of place and considered turning around. After a brief moment, I entered the door and I was greeted by the receptionist. She explained the process of checking and what was expected of me every day that I was present.

The first thing that we all did was gather up in a line and began to get weighed, one at a time. It felt crazy to me but this was the process of the center. Imagine how I felt. A black dot on a white piece of paper. I was the only African-American woman there and the only woman in her late 20's. I was leery about how this was going to work since I had nothing in common with the others. All through the process of getting weighed they were complaining like little children (which they were) and I began to get even more annoyed. It took everything in me not to say, "Shut up". But what right did I have to look at them differently when we were standing in the same line. I felt so humiliated and stupid. I had allowed my addiction to get so bad that this was the only place to turn. Disappointment in myself was an understatement. I had never felt so alone and out of place in my entire life. Tears began to fall down my face but I washed them away quickly with my hand because I could not allow for any of them to see my pain.

It took some time for me to get acclimated to the process, along with being the only Black woman. The days began to get harder but being in the treatment center around younger people began to get a little more bearable. As the different group sessions occurred I realized that they were struggling in the same manner that I was struggling. They were dealing with many of the same issues. The only difference was that they were able to begin their process of healing much earlier than me. They were provided with a head start on life and I had some catching up to do.

Growing up, I found that I have always been a watcher. I would look at people's actions and how they responded to life. One day while in the general group session I was watching each person in the room. I began to be amazed at what I saw. Every young woman there was chewing gum. Now you might say that there is nothing strange about that situation. As I continued to watch them they began to feed off of one another, asking for more gum. And then one girl stated that this is the only way that she could get a sugar rush without being watched and they all agreed. They had tons of gum in their pocketbooks and it was all because of the rush that sugar provided to their body and mind. I was so fascinated and relieved. For so long I thought that I was going insane for chewing so many pieces of gum at one time. It seems disgusted. But what I found out was that all of them there had an eating disorder and consumed tremendous amounts of gum to satisfy their craving for sugar. What an insightful moment for me. Just watching them, helped me to gain a better understanding of what we were all dealing with.

Now, even though I began to learn more about myself in understanding many of my actions, I continued to binge and purge on a daily basis. I thought that I buried these actions because I was at the funeral. I placed them in the casket and threw dirt over them. The problem was that I was not ready to deal with the loss and began to dig them back up the very next day. I was learning more about myself but not getting down to the nooks and crannies of what was causing all of this pain. I still did not feel comfortable enough to talk about the physical nor the sexual abuse in the open forums.

Throughout the many groups, art therapy gave me the best satisfaction. It also provided one of the biggest breakthroughs because I was able to recognize and give this disease a name. Art has always been a place of peace and healing for me. I love the sense of being able to create from the heart my thoughts and ideas and placing them on canvas. Whether it's done in the form of painting, drawing or the form of photography, it created healing in my heart, soul, and mind. So with all of that said, I was excited and could not wait for this class to occur. During this one session, we had to create what our disease resembled. What was it that we imagined? How did it manifest itself into our brains? How was it cultivated? This project was not hard for me to create. I have been so angry at it for so long that I knew actually what it resembled. It was a creation of a huge monster that was destroying my life and making me sicker than ever before. The eyes of the monster were hateful. Its soul was damaged and tormented. Its head consumed every part of my body making me believe that this was who I was 20 times over. It took away from the finances that were important to my home. It took away my health and could have taken my life.

It removed me from spending quality time with my family and placed a huge barrier within my marriage. Bulimia had turned my life upside down. This monster turned my life upside down. This thing had a force that controlled my every thought; therefore it was time for it to go. I don't appreciate being controlled especially since individuals had been controlling me since eight years old. Enough was enough!

Another day at the center and it was time to meet with the psychiatrist again. Medication was the topic of the day. Psychotropic medication seems to always be the answer for every ailment that has to do with mental instability. In our society medication seems to be the answer. There is no problem on earth that can be resolved by covering it up and that's how I saw the use of medication. It covers the symptoms but it does not fix the problem. I needed for my issues to be fixed; otherwise, I would have been living in that state of addiction for the rest of my life.

As I began to explain my fight to stay medication free, the psychiatrist was adamant about placing me on Zoloft. He strongly suggested that I take this medication to help with the depression levels. I was not too keen on this recommendation. The meeting was only the second time that we met and it was for less 30 minutes. Already he was suggesting that I take medication. Within this center, it seemed like a regular practice that everyone there was on some type of medication, but I refused. I made it very clear to him that I was not going to invade my system with an unknown drug that could affect my body negatively. I knew that it could alter my state of mind and I was not interested in having that happen. The psychiatrist did not argue with me but he still wrote out the prescription and told me to think about it.

Think about it! Think about changing how I moved throughout the course of the day. Think about how this could affect my sleep patterns and possibly put me in a stupor from the side effects of the drug. Medication has never sat well within my body and this was another fear that I had to decide if it was going to be helpful or a hindrance. The cons outweighed the pros in this situation.

Within my mind, I could not correlate the use of medication and end my addiction. I began to consult a few people in getting their opinion on taking medication. There were split analyses on what to do, which made me even more confused. I wanted to get better and was willing to do whatever it took to get there but invading my body with medication was incomprehensible to me. I fought with myself for weeks trying to get an understanding of why I might need this to help me. I kept working on the pro side of the list in hopes of swaying my argument of why I should not take them. I felt like I was losing my mind going back and forth within my brain. After fighting and getting tired I just wanted this whole process to be over. I knew that this doctor was not going to stop pushing for me to take them, so out of frustration and just wanting this to be over with, I decided to take the medication after three weeks of contemplation. I was embarrassed to get the prescription filled at the pharmacy. It felt like they were talking about me, but it was just me being paranoid. I tried to keep this a secret as much as possible. People tend to have a different perception of those on medication, and it is usually negative.

The first time that I took them I was nervous for the whole day. I didn't understand how fast they worked in the body. Even though the dosage was not very high, after a course of a few weeks it began to alter my mind and gave me a feeling that was not of myself. It made me feel strange and sometimes not present. What I noticed was that the medication did not stop me from purging or bingeing, so why did I need to take it. I did not understand the purpose of taking them. But for the sake of keeping the peace with my doctor and a few others, I continued to take them. When I left the center, I weaned myself off of them immediately.

For many people, medication serves its purpose. Fast forwarding to today as a therapist, I do understand the need for it. It has its place in a person's healing process, but it should not be the first thought in fixing our issues that we are facing. Within my healing, medication was not necessary and useless.

Medication is used for so many reasons. Through our physical healing as well as our mental healing it has a place to serve. In my opinion, medication should not be the first solution to a problem. As with any ailment, if we look at high blood or high cholesterol one of the first things some doctors prescribe is a change in a person's behavior. The doctor changes the person's diet, how they sleep along with the amount of exercise that is done on a daily basis before they prescribe anything for the most part. For the mind, behavior modifications should be examined first to see if the problem can be helped. Medication should be provided as a last resort and not the primary resolution. Let's just be more conscious about our health and what we put in our bodies. If we change our minds, we can change our behaviors.

Scare Tactic

Scare tactics are usually used to help individuals get their point across. Sometimes they work and other times they are seen as what they are, which is a tactic to put fear within an individual. During another meeting with the psychiatrist, he began to ask me about my behaviors in regards to bingeing and purging. I was honest about my behaviors in that they had not ceased. With this information, he decided to discuss the negative effects of using laxatives and how they could destroy my body. Destruction was not a word that I would have correlated with taking laxatives even though the amount that I took exceeded the prescribed amount. Yes, I did experience a tremendous amount of pain but logically I connected the pain with taking 30 laxatives at one time. I did not connect it to destroying my intestinal track.

Anyway, his discussions around the effects of laxatives were brief but hard. There was no sugar coating of the facts about what could happen if I continued to use laxatives in such a reckless manner. At this time in my life, I never knew what a Colostomy bag was until he began to get very detailed. In my case, its function would revolve around the intestines rupturing due to being on overload because of all the laxatives that consumed my body. The body waste would need to go through its regular form of excreting itself through the intestine in its proper manner. If the intestines burst, then the bag is used as the connector to the stomach so that a person's bowels can process from their body. The part that got me was being connected to the outside of the body. Vanity stepped in and I quickly began to see the big picture.

I did not want to be exposed to this type of trauma, all because I could not stop purging. An extreme amount of fear came over me and I began to think about my actions in a more serious way than before. Thoughts of having a bag full of body waste on the outside of my body got me to thinking. I will not lie and say that this totally changed my perception and at that moment I stopped. Believe me when I tell you that that did not occur. But I did begin to take my life a little more seriously and for the first time started to take my healing from this addiction with a different point of view.

Colostomy Bag!

Vanity!
Fear!
Enough to begin to change my thinking!

Who Can See What I see?

During my time at the center, I began to attend family therapy. I was nervous about this stage because it was no longer myself and the therapist. There were other thoughts within the room that made me feel uncomfortable and frustrated at times. Sometimes the other thoughts were challenging and made me feel not validated and at times the opposite occurred. There were times of disbelief in the room in regards to my feelings and why I did things. Some placed blame upon themselves, which is not what I was looking to do. Those sessions were not about me blaming others, but trying to get the ones close to me connected in heart, not just in body. Not always an easy task to accomplish.

Not everyone that I hoped to be in the groups showed up. Having them there was so important to me, but they did not feel the need to be involved. The pain that I felt was unbearable and unsupported. At one of the biggest times of my life that I needed their support, they failed me. I questioned for a long time, why didn't he support me. My own flesh and blood left me to fend for myself. It took me some time to get over this, but I did have to let it go. The healing that I was seeking could not be interrupted because of what he did or did not do for me. So I had to swallow a big girl pill and walk this walk without him.

Also within the group dynamics, there was a tendency by other family members to place their perception on me which were hurtful because many times they were not true to form. I never understood how individuals could take their perceptions and make it true for my life. But when I tried to explain my position it was seen so small and their thoughts were seen so large.

How could that be? We all have doubts and fears within our life and many times if we have not dealt with our stuff we will push it on to someone else to bear. Not a good practice for individuals that are suffering.

Lastly, I was so annoyed with family therapy and I just wanted it to be over with. Within family therapy, there was a session where it was just the therapist and myself because no one could come. On this one occasion, we had a discussion with me being an African-American woman. He stated that he did not understand why I was there due to his belief of Black women loving their curves. He was a little less conservative and more focused on the size of our butts and our breast. Why was this White man talking to me about what Black women like? I must have given him a strange look because he asked me what was wrong. After a while he informed me that his wife was Black and how she liked being voluptuous, therefore every Black woman is that way. At that moment I realized that this man had no idea what being Bulimic was all about. What did my curves have to do with having an eating disorder? He was clueless and therefore made me very angry. From that point on I was not interested in what he had to say. Thankfully my time at the center was almost up because he did not make any sense to me at all. Every therapist is not a match for everybody and he was not a match for me.

What a huge misconception. Why are we as black women put in this box and all made to look the same? I struggle with the thoughts of society believing that we all think that same. And to have a professional say this to me was hurtful and unprofessional. We have to understand that having an eating disorder goes way beyond a curve on your body. It is a mental disruption in your mind that is seeking to be complete and even if I had what some would say a perfect body that would not have cured me. We need to recognize our struggles and find the proper help and not allow society to place us in a box.

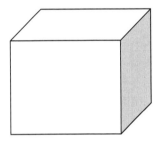

Big Body!
Big Butt!
Big Lips!
Big Boned Boxes!

We are individuals! Not Boxes!
As Black Women, it takes us some time to seek out the help!
We need the same kindness and understanding that is given to others, be given to us.

Tie Breakers!

Within my treatment at the center, I had to see a Nutritionist and an individual Therapist. The Nutritionist was a breath of fresh air since she was the only face that looked like mine. She was tough but honest, hard but real, feisty but compassionate. I hated her at first because she forced me to eat things that I did not want to eat. All of my life I had been a picky eater. If my food didn't look right I would not eat it, if it didn't smell right, I would not eat. And I am the same way today. But she did not care about what I wanted but was more concerned about what I needed to be healthy. She forced me to begin to look at myself and see the goodness that was invisible in my own eyes. She talked to me as if I was an adult that needed to give myself a break. Even though she hounded me on a daily basis, she made me feel as if this disease could be conquered and destroyed. She was like a sergeant in the service giving orders and standing by the bathroom door making sure that no one purged. And before you went into the bathroom you could not take your pocketbook and she would check your pockets for any pills. She was rough but for some reason, she became one of the best parts of me being there. This beautiful Black woman became a huge part of my healing and it was about time. She was concerned about me and I was thankful. She got it! She understood!

As one of the last requirements within the center, I had to attend one on one therapy. Such a great experience because my therapist listened with an open heart and understood the disease as a whole. Therefore I was not judged by being a Black woman in the treatment center. I was given a lot of respect and not looked upon as weird for being at the center. I allowed myself to begin to open up about my past as a child, being a survivor of childhood sexual abuse and discussing the physical abuse. We were able to make breakthroughs that no other session could do. It began to release my fears of the past and started to usher me into the new life that I could be free of this disease one day. Also within our session, she would give me homework to complete. Some of the assignment included other family members to be a part which did not always happen. There was one assignment where I had to write a letter and send it to this particular family member. It was someone that was extremely close to me and by sending this letter to them I was hoping for validation. I really had high hopes that even though they did not attend any of my sessions, I thought that maybe, just maybe they would respond to the letter. Well, you probably know by now that they never responded. Never! They never said one word about what was happening in my life. It made me feel unimportant. The pain consumed me for a while. I kept going through different scenarios in my head of how I could have approached him about the topic, but I was never successful. What I realized was that I had to come to terms with his lack of support for me and I no longer relied on how other people responded to my pain to be set free. I no longer gave control to them. So I had to let it go within myself and move forward. I would be lying if I said that I never worried about why they didn't respond, but I loved them very much, and I had to let it go.

So the time had come for me to leave. 90 days had passed and it was time to see if I could make it on my own. Towards the end of my stay, I did have some success while being at the center. One of the most important pieces was that I stopped using laxatives and buried them for good. I was really afraid of losing my bowls on the outside and even more I was afraid of dying if they were to burst. This time the funeral was full of joy and the tears were full of the thoughts about the time that I had wasted on giving up on myself. The downside was that the bingeing did not stop at the same time but through constant healing and working on myself it also dissipated eventually. I no longer gave up on me but began to fight for my rights as a human being and decided that I wanted to live in a more peaceful and healthy manner. So all in all, going to the center was the perfect thing to do and it ended up helping me to get stronger. It was not the medication that did it but the kindness, the openness and the truth that consumed them that worked there, therefore brought healing to my life. I no longer allowed myself to stay a victim and finally allowed myself to become a survivor. What an amazing defeat for someone to conquer? I would have never thought that I could get to this place of healing. I wanted to live for the first time in my life. I saw purpose in me, I saw the passion in me, and I saw the desire in me. I was excited about what I could do in this world and I realized that I did have support and that I was not alone anymore. How awesome was that? Extremely!!!

Eating Disorders have been such a prevalent part of our world for women, men, and children. We are so focused in this country on thinness that it has disturbed many individuals' lives to the point of death. Even with that, many people continue to perpetuate the importance of being thin therefore our youth continues to aspire to those negative images. We continue to place stigmas on people that are 5, 10 or even 30 pounds over what we consider to look good in society. How can that be? How can the world dictate what looks attractive and what does not look attractive? And how can we as a human race allow that to continue with all of the harm that it has done?

Anorexia
A) Fear of becoming fat or obese even when weight is normal.
B) Rejection of normal weight in relation to age and weight.
C) Perception disturbances in relation to body self-image.
D) Amenorrhea. (4)

Bulimia
A) Binge eating: (frequent episodes)
    1) In a short period (less than 2 h) or in more quantity of food than desirable.
    2) Feeling of losing control over eating.
B) Compensatory behaviors such as excessive exercise vomit, and the use of diuretics or medicines.
C) Both, binge eating and compensatory behaviors at least during 3 months and no less than twice per week.

D) Self-concept or evaluation depends extremely on body image and weight. These behaviors not only occur during an anorectic episode or disorder. (4)

EDNOS (Eating Disorder Not Otherwise Specified)
1) All criteria for anorexia are present, but amenorrhea is absent.
2) Weight responds to normal expectations.
3) All criteria for bulimia are present, but not at the same frequency.
4) The patient affect compensatory behaviors even if weight is normal but they do not have binge eating.
5) They chew and spit the food, they do not swallow.
6) Binge eating is present, but compensatory behaviors are not present. (4)

Affirmations are positive words that you think and say to yourself. Below are some affirmations to help aid in your healing process. Our words can dictate how we function and live our lives. So if we speak life into our world than goodness has to come forth.

1. I am beautiful.
2. I can do all things through Christ that Strengthen me.
3. I can climb the highest mountain.
4. I have conquered this addiction.
5. I am what God said that I am.
6. I believe in myself.
7. I trust myself.
8. I am in Love with myself.
9. There is hope in this life.
10. I am set free from all hurt and pain.
11. Life is amazing.
12. My weight has nothing to do with my self-worth.
13. I deserve the best out of life.
14. I have the biggest heart.
15. I embrace the world and all its greatness.
16. I will be good to myself and others.
17. I am no longer helpless
18. I am no longer a victim but a survivor.
19. I am life.
20. I love my body.
21. I am my own unique individual covered in God's love.
22. I am at peace with oneself.
23. I am a gift from God and I will not be ashamed.
24. I am the righteousness of God.
25. I am perfect.

One of the biggest issues with having an eating disorder is that many times we go through it alone. We usually do not have a buddy to binge with because it's embarrassing, it's humiliating and it's disgusting. We tend to isolate ourselves to the point of extreme depression and many times suicide. In order to be healed, we have to take some prevalent steps.

1.   Find your Spirituality- All through the land, there are many religions. People depend on different things to get them through in needing something to believe. Well, all through this book I was not ashamed to tell you my belief system that got me through, which is Christianity. I am a true and firm believer in Jesus Christ our Lord and Savior. He has gotten me through every day of my life and this is where my hope and faith lies. And I pray that whoever finds where your hope and faith lies because you deserve it.

2.   Find some Support (Friend and/or Family) - We all need someone that we can talk to and trust. That one person that is not going to judge us or make fun of us for our behaviors. That one person that is filled with compassion and love and is willing to listening when you need them. In this disease, we have spent enough time alone and now it is time to be free and the sooner you come out from behind it, the sooner you can begin to get healed.

3.   Find Professional Help- Professional help was the best thing that I could have ever done for myself. It could be that you might have to check into a treatment center or seek out a therapist or psychologist that's trained in working with eating disorder patients. Give yourself a chance to live and get healthy for yourself. We all have gifts and if we lose ourselves we will not be able to give that special gift to the world.

Also, seek out medical help from your general doctor for a full physical to make sure that nothing is damaged. And if there is damage at least you are in the right place to receive help. We have to take care of our bodies inside and out. Get healed completely.

4.   Self-Care – We have to begin to take care of ourselves physically, mentally, emotionally and spiritually. We have to begin to learn to eat better, therefore, seeing a nutritionist could be very helpful. Drinking a lot of water is necessary for our total well-being (1/2 of our body weight is how many ozs. we should drink a day). Allowing ourselves to breathe from our stomach allows for the oxygen to circulate through our bodies. Giving ourselves time to do something fun is great for our mental and emotional health. And last but most important seeking out God for total healing. We must believe in ourselves in all that we do.

5.   Journaling- This has been a great source of healing for me and can allow you to speak from your heart in a safe way. It can provide an outlet so that your mind can be free of all of those thoughts that continue to run through the mind when it is confusing. Find yourself a book that is creative and beautiful to enjoy. Allow the color to bring you alive within yourself.

Always remember that you are not alone in your recovery. You do not have to hurt in silence but allow yourself to be free. Seek deep down inside of yourself and don't be ashamed to speak about your past. It's your golden key to your future.

Scene 4

My New Day

As I reflect on my life, God has blessed me tremendously. He has brought me so far that I don't even recognize the woman that I am today. She is unfamiliar to me. I was that broken little girl unable to express herself in a positive way. Unable to care for herself, therefore used negative coping skills to handle the stressors of life. I allowed the world to entangle me in all of its problems. I took everything that the world said to me and made it my truth. One the biggest questions that I am asked often is: how did I make it? And the only way that I know how to respond to that is to tell them the name, Jesus. There is no other explanation of how someone in so much turmoil could make it out of that mess. Being reborn allows for me to give my knowledge back to others. It is such a great feeling to bring about a change in other people's life. It's no longer about me but about helping others. People are starving for knowledge, people are starving to be heard, and people are starving to be seen. So, with that, I am doing all that I can to bring a sense of awareness to anyone who wants and desires to have it.

Even though my life started out hard I have been blessed with two beautiful children. They are full of joy and laughter that feels my spirit on a daily basis. It's amazing how at one time, I never thought that motherhood was for me. But now I can't imagine being anything other than a mother. It's a great gift and if you have the opportunity to be afforded children please do not take this blessing lightly.

Yes, it can be very challenging at times but you work through them. Our children are a reflection of us and if we give our best it will be given back to us in return. And one other great thing about being a mother is that I am now a grandmother and I call him Pumpkin. He is so adorable and he brings joy to my heart every time I get to see his smile. What a great gift of life and I pray that they never have to endure what I endured all of those many years.

In my first book, I talked about being married and how God renewed us. Well, we lived our life as we knew how and on February of 2013 he passed away from Lung cancer and it was hard for us to manage as a family. But we stuck together through this tragedy. It taught me a lot about life, love, commitment and just being open with my feelings. I took care of him when his body started to deteriorate due to cancer metastasizing all throughout his body and I was blessed with the opportunity to be by his side and be at home with him while he died. It was some of the most incredible days along with some of the most horrible days. But it was something that I will never forget. On February 16th, 2013 he died in my arms, in our living room. We were both prepared for his death but it was still hard to watch him wilt away. I never thought that I would have ever been able to recover from that trauma, but I did. I have been blessed to be able to move forward and love again.

Today I am married to an amazing man that loves me for me. He is the first man that knows all about my past, from the child sexual abuse, the domestic violence, the addictions along with the knowledge of infidelity. Yes, he has accepted me for me with no judgments. He is not perfect, to say the least, but he is perfect for me. See God provides us with opportunities to love again and to get it right. He provides us with the ability to love and forgive ourselves. He is just so awesome in every way and I am grateful.

One of the downfalls sometimes in experiencing so much trauma is that it can manifest itself in your body and cause sickness. A few years ago I was diagnosed with Lupus, Mixed Connective Tissue Disease, and Fibromyalgia. All of these diseases attack the muscles and nervous system. It has been a rough road due to the constant pain that I am in on a daily basis. So remember I talked about my hesitation to taking medication, well I have gotten used to it because the pain is that bad. And because I take the medication it does help to decrease the pain sometime. But I am pushing through every day because it's necessary. So some days are filled with tears because it's hard to move. And other days are good and I take advantage of them. Having these diagnoses is just another part of the process. It's not a death sentence, it's just what happens and my strength gets stronger every day.

For many years I had no idea what I wanted to do with my life. After being expelled from college I was so unsure about my future. As time flew by I began to get discouraged and therefore had to develop a plan for my life, so I began searching in many different areas. I attended school to become an EMT but that did not work out. When it came to taking the state test I was unable to the past and I never tried again. I attended school to become a Real Estate Broker but that did not work out either. Once again, I took the exam and I failed. Lastly, I attended technical school to become a Paralegal which was successful. The problem was that when I went to find a job it was not easy to obtain due to no experience. It took years later for me to realize what my goals and dreams consisted of, therefore I attended community college and received my Associates Degree in Liberal Arts/Sciences.

This degree helped to advance me a little but it did not fulfill that hole within me. Two years later, I attended Thomas Edison and received my Bachelor's Degree. After that, I began to put together a plan that included, becoming a therapist so therefore the plan was set and ready to be worked out. So I attended Capella University and received my Master's Degree in Counseling Psychology. After I graduated I was promoted as a Therapist providing a service to survivors of domestic violence, sexual abuse, who are struggling with mental health issues. There was a time where I was not mature enough to do the work that I do. So with that said my maturity level has developed in a way that allows me to handle all that is in my path, therefore, nothing can stop me now. I am also a Director at my current job where I am over our Sexual Abuse and Domestic Violence programs. It's very rewarding to be able to give back a piece of me.

I know that in my last book I discussed also going to school for my PH.D. Well after five years of school I no longer deemed it necessary. It started to feel like I was doing this for everyone else and not for myself. I began to hate the process and it was no longer fun for me. It felt like a job, so I stopped. I completed all of my coursework, just not my dissertation which would have extended another two years. So I gave myself permission to stop. For the first time, I gave myself permission to respond to my needs and not the needs of others. Sometimes we have to realize that it's ok to take care of ourselves. Yah for me! And can I tell you that I felt so relieved when I had to make that huge decision. It was right for me to do at that time and I have no regrets. So never forget to do what is right for you. That's what's important.

Another big event occurred in my life which was starting my own non-profit organization called Healing Wounds…Changing the Lives of Others. This organization is based out of Camden County which serves survivors of sexual abuse and domestic violence. There are many services along our great state but there are not many services that serve underserved population well. So that's part of my goal in serving my community well. We provide group sessions and training in many areas to help educate our communities around social injustices. I am so grateful to give back in this way and will continue to be an advocate for those that are hurting and suffering.

Another great piece was that God elevated me to become ordained as an Elder at my church, Renaissance Church Ministries in Sicklerville, NJ. It has been such an honor to witness for the Lord and the best thing that could ever happen to me. God has brought me full circle in that he took all of my hurt and pain and is allowing me to help others that are going through the same thing. I would have never thought in a million years that my life would be this full of joy and peace. I never thought that light existed for me. I truly believed that I was exempt from light shining upon me, but when you follow Christ and all of His wisdom, light has to shine. It removes every ounce of pain and suffering ever felt in one's life.

God, I am so grateful to you for being so wonderful to me. You have blessed my life, you have forgiven all my sins and you have been the best Father that anyone could ever ask for.

So with this book, I salute you!

- HealingWounds...Changing The Lives of Others
tamu.lane@yahoo.com Email
856-536-4972

- National Network to End Domestic Violence
2001 S. Street NW, Suite 400
Washington, DC 20009
202-543-5566

- The Women Center
1201 New Road
Linwood NJ 08221
609-601-9925
www.acwc.org

- Information for Victims of Crime
1-866-872-4973

- National Domestic Violence Hotline
1-800-799-SAFE

- New Jersey Coalition to End Domestic Violence
609-584-8107
TTY: 609-584-0027
Njcbw.org

- Child Abuse Hotline
1-877-652-2873
TTY: 1-800-835-5510

- RAINN (Rape Abuse and Incest National Network
www.SafeHelpLine.org
RAINN.org
National Sexual Abuse Hotline

1-800-656-HOPE

- Childhelp National Child Abuse Hotline
1-800-4-A-CHILD

- Sexual Assault Resource Agency
www.sexualassaultresources.rog/
SARA 24-Hour Hotline 434-977-7273

- National Eating Disorder Association
www.nationaleatingdisorders.org/get-help
NEDA Helpline: 1-800-931-2237

- Eating Disorder Hotline
www.eatingdisorderhotline.com/
877-377-7741

- National Association of Anorexia Nervosa and
Associated Disorders, Inc.
Helpline: 630-577-1330

- National Suicide Prevention Lifeline-
1-800-273-TALK

References Bibliography

(1)   Diagnostic and Statistical Manual of Mental Disorders (DSM-IV)

(2)   The Center for Disease Control and Prevention. 2010 Summary Report.

http://www.cdc.gov/violenceprevention/nisvs/index.html

(3)The Holy Bible (KJV)

(4)   Guinzbourg, M., (2011) Eating Disorders – A Current Concern Similarities and Differences Among the Anorexia, Bulimia, and EDNOS Categories. Rorschachiana, 2011, Volume 32, pp. 2-45. DOI: 10.1027/1192-5604/a000014

(5)   Department of Justice, Office of Justice Programs, Bureau of Justice Statistics, National Crime Victimization Survey, 2010-2014 (2015).

(6)   Department of Justice, Office of Justice Programs, Bureau of Justice Statistics, Sex Offenses and Offenders (1997).

(7)   Childhood Sexual Abuse, Teenage Pregnancy, and Partnering with Adult Men: Exploring the Relationship Holly M. Harner, RNC, PhD, MPH Journal of Psychosocial Nursing and Mental Health Services. 2005; 43 (8): 20-28HTTPS:10.3928/02793695-20050801-09

About the Author

Tamu Lane is 45 years old and is happily married to Jason Lane. She has two children and one grandson. Tamu currently has her own non-profit organization called Healing Wounds...Changing the Lives of Others in hopes of bringing about a change within her community and in the world. She sees this as a true blessing from God. She was able to take her past and make it a bright future around the years of painful experiences. This was only God working this out in her favor and she is thankful. She is no longer distraught about her past and is excited to share a piece of her life with the world.

Please grab a hold to it and don't let it go. It could save your life or the life of a loved one.

Made in the USA
San Bernardino, CA
16 March 2018